You're OVERWATERING it!

A plant guru's guide to houseplants

Jonny Balchandani
@thebeardedplantaholic

EBURY PRESS

INTRODUCTION:
Welcome to the Jungle 6

LEVEL 1: PLANT NOOB

Chapter 1: Choosing Your Starter Plants and Misleading Advice 15

Chapter 2: The Right Plant for the Right Jungle 23

LEVEL 2: BUDDING BOTANIST

Chapter 3: Understanding Light Requirements 31

Chapter 4: Watering Wisdom 40

Chapter 5: Soil and the Living Ecosystem 47

LEVEL 3: PLANT GUARDIAN

Chapter 6: Nutrient Know-How 59

Chapter 7: Pest Patrol 67

Chapter 8: Propagation – Growing Your Collection for Free 75

LEVEL 4: ADVANCED CULTIVATOR

Chapter 9: Humidity and Air Quality – the Unseen Lifeline of Your Jungle 85

Chapter 10: Dealing with Plant Stress 93

Chapter 11: Seasonal Plant Care – Does It Even Matter? 101

LEVEL 5: PLANT WHISPERER

Chapter 12: Specialty Plant Care – Divas, Survivors and the Unapologetically Weird 111

Chapter 13: Pruning and Training and Going Full Jungle Mode 119

Chapter 14: Repotting and Root Care – Digging Deep Into Plant Survival 127

Chapter 15: Sustainable Plant Care – Keeping Your Jungle Green (for Real) 135

Chapter 16: The Art of Plant Displays – Designing a Living Masterpiece 143

LEVEL 6: PLANT CURATOR

Chapter 17: The Plant Curator's Guide to Rare Finds 151

Chapter 18: The Jungle Doctor's Guide to Extreme Plant Rehab 159

LEVELLING UP:
From Jungle Boss to Plant Mystic 168

Chapter 19: Plant Science Demystified – Unlocking the Jungle Code 171

Chapter 20: When Plants Go Rogue 177

Chapter 21: The Secret Underground Life Beneath the Pot 183

Chapter 22: The Anatomy of Growth 191

Chapter 23: Taming the Wild 199

Chapter 24: Plant Sentience 207

CONGRATULATIONS, JUNGLE GURU! 215

YOU WEREN'T ALWAYS A PLANT PERSON NEITHER WAS I

I didn't start this journey as some mystical, green-fingered wizard. There was no grand awakening in a lush rainforest, no spiritual moment where I whispered to a fern and it whispered back. Nope. I started with a single pothos.

A scrappy little vine. That's it. A plant so forgiving, so ridiculously unkillable, that it practically thrives on neglect. And even then, I still managed to screw it up at first. Overwatered it. Underwatered it. Moved it around too much. Left it for dead and then, miraculously, watched it bounce back like some botanical cockroach. That pothos didn't just survive – it sparked something.

It made me look at plants differently. Not as décor. Not as an aesthetic. But as living things with their own needs, instincts and behaviours.

And like all good obsessions, it escalated. Hard.

That pothos led to a few more plants. Then a few more. Then suddenly, my home wasn't a home anymore – it was a living, breathing jungle. A place where plants climbed the walls, cascaded from shelves and wrapped themselves around every available surface.

I went from 'guy who owns a couple of plants' to full-blown plant addict.

I learnt everything I could. Studied how plants grow, how they communicate, how they survive. I experimented, propagated, hacked together new methods. And yeah – I killed a lot of plants along the way. A lot. But each mistake made me better. Every failure was a lesson.

And at some point, I realised something:

Most of the plant advice out there is absolute nonsense.

Water your plant every 7 days? Rubbish.

Misting increases humidity? Barely.

All plants go dormant in winter? Not if you control their environment.

And don't even get me started on the 'just put an ice cube on your orchid' people. You monsters.

So, I started sharing what I'd learnt. The real, field-tested knowledge that actually makes a difference. The hacks, the tricks, the science

– but without the boring, textbook approach. People resonated with it. And before I knew it, I wasn't just some guy with a house full of plants anymore. I was TheBeardedPlantaholic.

I went viral. Not just for my plant knowledge, but for my no-BS, straight-talking approach to plant care. No sugarcoating. No overcomplicating. Just practical, honest plant advice – with a generous dose of sarcasm, of course.

WHY THIS BOOK?

You don't need another fluffy, feel-good, Pinterest-perfect houseplant guide. You need a training manual. A gritty, no-nonsense handbook that teaches you how to actually understand your plants – so you don't just keep them alive but get them to thrive.

This book is for the people who are done guessing, done killing plants and done falling for bad advice. Whether you're a total beginner or someone who's been at this for a while, this book will take your plant game to the next level.

By the time you turn the last page, you'll know how to:

- Read your plants like a pro – because yes, they do talk (just not in words).

- Dodge the most common plant-killing mistakes (looking at you, serial overwaterers).

- Propagate, rescue and turn your jungle into an actual ecosystem.

- Troubleshoot everything from yellowing leaves to root rot like a jungle doctor.

- Stop treating plants like decoration and start treating them like the complex, intelligent organisms they are.

WHAT THIS BOOK ISN'T

It's not for people who just want to buy a plant and forget about it.

It's not a 'water once a week' generic care guide.

It's not going to sugarcoat things – some plants are divas, some are nearly indestructible and some will throw a tantrum no matter what you do.

This book is for the ones who actually give a damn. For those who want to learn, experiment and truly connect with their plants.

WHAT YOU'RE ABOUT TO GET INTO

This isn't just a book about how to care for plants – it's a book about understanding them. Because once you understand your plants, plant care stops being a chore and starts becoming second nature.

And it's not just about the plants. It's about you.

Because if there's one thing I've learnt, it's this:

Growing plants changes you.

It teaches you patience. It forces you to slow down and notice the small things. It sparks creativity. And sometimes, it even changes the way you see the world.

If you let it, this journey will be about more than just leaves and roots. It'll be about transformation.

So, are you ready to become a Jungle Boss?

LEVEL 1
PLANT NOOB

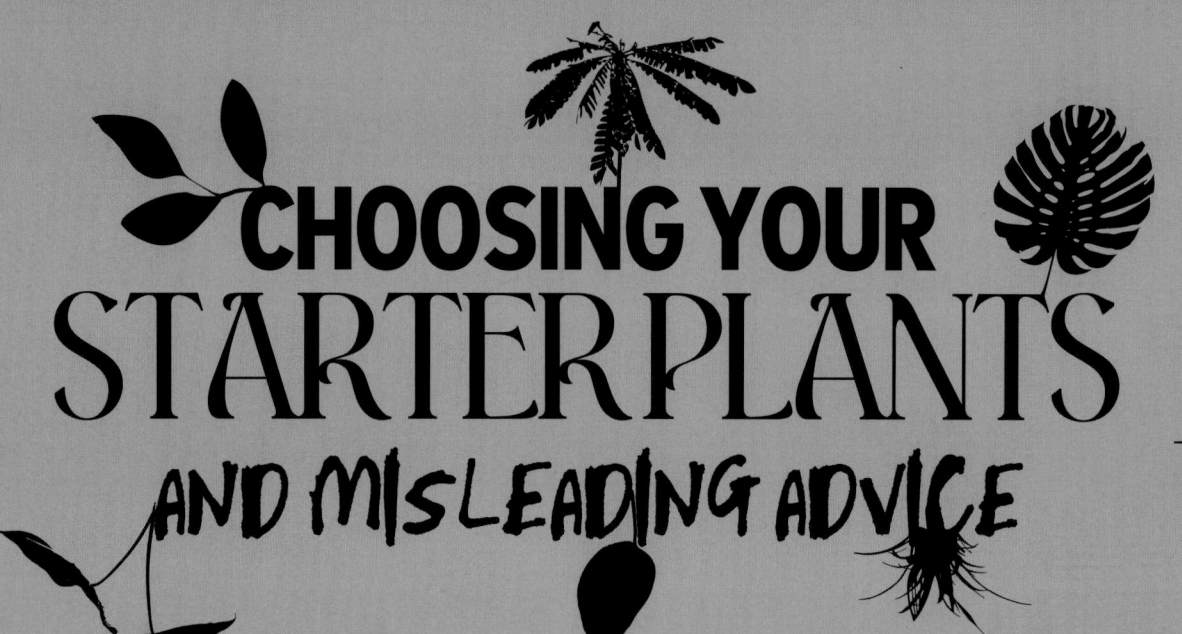

CHOOSING YOUR STARTER PLANTS AND MISLEADING ADVICE

THE BULLSH*T THEY TELL YOU AND THE PLANTS THAT WON'T BETRAY YOU

Let's start with a hard truth: not all plants want to live.

Some are built for survival, ready to thrive in your care no matter what you throw at them. Others? They exist purely to test your patience and crush your spirit.

Yet, if you waltz into any garden centre, you'll find misleading labels and bad advice steering unsuspecting new plant parents straight into heartbreak. Plants with reputations for being 'easy' that are, in fact, divas in disguise. Care instructions that are so ridiculously vague, they may as well just say: 'Good luck, sucker.'

So, before we get to the real MVPs – the plants that actually have your back – let's talk about the biggest traps, myths and marketing scams designed to part you from your money and leave you surrounded by dying leaves.

THE TRAP OF HOUSEPLANT LABELS: LIES, DECEPTION AND MISLEADING ADVICE

You've seen them. Those innocent-looking labels that come with every plant you buy. A tiny plastic tag promising foolproof care instructions, usually with a name, a symbol of a sun, a little water droplet and something vague like 'keep soil moist'.

Sounds simple, right? Too bad it's all nonsense.

WHY HOUSEPLANT LABELS ARE A SCAM

Here's the problem: labels don't know where you live. They don't know your light levels. They don't know your humidity. They don't know that you have the memory of a goldfish when it comes to watering. Yet they'll tell you to water 'once a week' like it's some kind of universal truth. Some labels don't even have the right plant name on them. Yes, really.

THE BIGGEST LIES ON HOUSEPLANT LABELS

'Water once a week' – the worst advice ever

This is the biggest crime against beginner plant parents. No one can tell you exactly when to water a plant without knowing:

- What kind of soil it's in.
- What size the pot is.
- How much airflow it gets.
- How humid your home is.
- How much light it gets.

A plant in a tiny plastic nursery pot in a hot, dry room will dry out in days. The same plant in a big ceramic pot in a cool, shady corner? Might take two weeks or more to need water.

Better strategy? Stick your finger in the soil. If it's dry 5 cm (2 inches) down, water. If it's damp, step away from the watering can.

'Low light' doesn't mean what you think

Here's a secret: most plants sold as 'low light' will survive in low light, not thrive.

They'll slow down, stop growing, stretch and eventually throw a fit if they're left in a dark corner for too long. 'Low light' in a garden centre doesn't mean 'stick it in your windowless bathroom and forget about it'. It means 'tolerates a bright room, but away from direct sun'. And don't even get me started on succulents labelled 'indoor plants' when they need blazing hot sun to survive.

The name game: mislabelled plants and identity crises

Another fun scam: mislabelled plants. You pick up something labelled 'philodendron', but it's actually a pothos, or an aloe that's actually an agave, and suddenly you're treating a desert plant like a houseplant and wondering why it's dying. Or – worst of all – a majesty palm labelled 'easy care' (spoiler: it's not).

Rule #1 of plant shopping: always double-check the name. Look it up, use a plant ID app or ask someone who knows their stuff. If the name seems vague or generic? Be suspicious.

THE PERSONALITY TEST: WHAT KIND OF PLANT PARENT ARE YOU?

Not all beginner plant parents are the same. Some of you are born nurturers, others are chaos incarnate. Let's figure out what kind of plant parent you are and match you with the right **LEAFY COMPANION**.

THE 'SET IT AND FORGET IT' SURVIVOR

Traits: You want plants, but let's be real – you forget they exist half the time. You need a plant that thrives on neglect.

Your Perfect Match:

- **Snake Plant** – Will tolerate being ignored for weeks and still look fabulous. Pictured below.
- **ZZ Plant** – Almost impossible to kill. The cockroach of houseplants (in the best way).

THE OVERBEARING PLANT HELICOPTER PARENT

Traits: You check on your plants like they're newborn babies, obsess over every yellowing leaf and might be watering too much out of love.

Your Perfect Match:

- **Calathea** – Demands constant attention. A drama queen that needs your care.
- **Alocasia** – As fussy as you are. If you love high-maintenance relationships, this one's for you. *Alocasia* 'Loco' pictured below.

THE EXPERIMENTAL SCIENTIST

Traits: You don't just own plants – you're running a full-blown botanical experiment. Propagating, air-layering, growing in LECA (see page 48) … you're always testing something.

Your Perfect Match:

- **Pothos** – The easiest propagator in the game. Perfect for endless cuttings. Golden pothos pictured to the right.
- **Anthurium** – Get into the world of fancy foliage and watch how they change under different conditions.

THE JUNGLE ARCHITECT

Traits: You're not just collecting plants – you're building a rainforest. Every corner must be green, every shelf must be full and you're already researching grow lights.

Your Perfect Match:

- *Monstera deliciosa* – A statement plant that rewards you with massive, iconic leaves. *Monstera deliciosa* 'Aurea Variegata' pictured above.
- *Epipremnum pinnatum* **'Cebu Blue'** – A fast-growing climber that will fill your space with cascading vines.

THE 'WHOOPS, I FORGOT' PLANT PARENT

Traits: You get excited about plants, but let's be honest, half the time you forget to water them until they start looking crispy.

Your Perfect Match:

- **Spider plant** – Will forgive you for occasional neglect and bounce back instantly. Pictured to the right.
- **Jade plant** – Stores water in its leaves like a succulent camel.

**FINAL THOUGHTS:
TRUST YOUR INSTINCTS, NOT THE LABELS**

The plant industry is filled with bad advice. Marketing gimmicks and generic care labels do not take into account your home, your light or your ability to remember to water things.

The secret to real success? Start with plants that WANT to live.

Choose plants that thrive, not just survive. Build your confidence, learn how to read your plants and by the time you're ready for the high-maintenance divas, you'll actually know what you're doing.

Because trust me – a thriving jungle of 'basic' plants feels a hell of a lot better than a shelf full of expensive, crispy divas.

So, choose wisely.

Your plant journey starts now

THE RIGHT PLANT FOR THE RIGHT JUNGLE

BRINGING HOME A PLANT IS EASY. KEEPING IT ALIVE? THAT'S WHERE THINGS GET INTERESTING.

If you've ever killed a plant before, you might have gone looking for an 'easy' one next – something marketed as unkillable. Maybe a ZZ plant, a snake plant or (God forbid) a peace lily because the garden centre employee swore it was 'low-maintenance' (spoiler: it's not). But here's the trap of so-called easy plants:

Just because a plant survives doesn't mean you'll actually enjoy taking care of it.

People often grab the first plant they're told is 'good for beginners' without stopping to think – *Do I even like this plant*? If you don't care about it, you won't enjoy the process. And when you stop caring? That's when plants actually die.

So, before you even think about what's 'easy', let's start with the real first question: what plant will make you want to keep it alive?

STEP ONE: CHOOSE A PLANT YOU ACTUALLY LIKE

Forget what's 'beginner-friendly' for a second. Imagine looking at your plant every day – does it make you excited to care for it? Would you be gutted if it died? That's the one you should get. Because the best beginner plant is the one you'll actually pay attention to.

Here's the formula for a great starter plant:

- It can handle a few mistakes (because let's be real, you're going to mess up at some point).
- It grows visibly so you actually feel like you're making progress.
- It suits your home's light and humidity – plants don't adapt to you, you adapt to them.
- You like it enough to care about it.

Without that last point, none of the others matter.

STEP TWO: KNOW YOUR HOME'S JUNGLE CONDITIONS

Before you pick a plant, take 5 minutes to check out your space. Every home has a unique microclimate – a mix of light, temperature, humidity and airflow – that makes or breaks a plant's survival.

This is where the Four Pillars of Plant Care come in – Light, Water, Soil and Humidity.

- **Light** – Can your plant actually 'see' the sky? Plants need to see the sky to thrive. If a plant has no direct or indirect access to daylight, it's already struggling (see page 31).
- **Water** – Are you the type to forget watering for weeks, or do you drown plants in love? Pick accordingly (see page 40).
- **Soil** – A plant's foundation. If the roots are in crap, the plant will be too (see page 47).
- **Humidity and airflow** – Is your home dry like a desert, humid like a jungle or somewhere in between (see page 85)?

Once you know your space, you can match your plant to it, instead of setting yourself up for failure.

Aglaonema 'Silver Bay'

THE PERSONALITY TEST: WHAT'S YOUR PLANT SOULMATE?

Alright, let's find your perfect first plant based on your home and your habits – because not every plant fits every space.

THE 'I WANT A PLANT THAT REFUSES TO DIE' CREW

Maybe you're new to this, or maybe you just need a plant that will thrive even when you forget it exists. You need a survivor – something low-maintenance, resilient and unbothered by neglect.

Best Picks:

- **Aspidistra (cast-iron plant)** – If a plant could have 'indestructible' as a personality trait, it would be this one. Survives in low light, low humidity and with inconsistent watering. Pictured below.

- ***Aglaonema* spp. (Chinese evergreen)** – Looks fancy but is secretly one of the easiest plants to own. Thrives in low light, tolerates missed waterings and comes in loads of wild colours.

- ***Rhaphidophora tetrasperma* (mini monstera)** – A fast-growing climber that looks expensive but is hard to kill.

Avoid: Fussy plants like orchids, alocasias and anything with 'princess' in the name.

THE 'I LOVE A BIT OF DRAMA' GANG

You enjoy nurturing your plants, and you don't mind a challenge. These plants will punish you for getting it wrong, but when you get it right? They'll reward you with insane beauty.

Best Picks:

- ***Calathea* 'Medallion'** – The drama queen of houseplants. Gorgeous patterned leaves, but hates tap water, dry air and sudden changes.

- ***Alocasia* 'Polly'** – An alien-looking beauty with striking leaves, but if you overwater, it'll drop them out of spite.

- ***Anthurium clarinervium*** – If you love velvet-textured leaves and high-maintenance care, this plant is your VIP ticket to the tropical elite. Pictured below.

Avoid: Cacti, succulents and pothos – you'll get bored.

THE 'I WANT BIG, LEAFY JUNGLE VIBES' CREW

You're here to turn your home into a rainforest. You want fast-growing, oversized foliage that makes your space feel like an indoor jungle.

Best Picks:

- *Monstera deliciosa* – The iconic jungle plant, known for its massive, fenestrated leaves.

- *Philodendron gloriosum* – Creeps across the soil like a jungle beast, growing massive, velvety leaves.

- *Syngonium* **'Albo'** – Variegated (see page 78) and fast-growing with arrow-shaped leaves that add serious character. Pictured below.

Avoid: Slow-growing plants like ZZ plants – they won't give you the lush jungle vibe you're after.

THE 'I'M OBSESSED WITH ODDITIES' SQUAD

If normal plants bore you and you want the rarest, weirdest foliage possible, this is your lane. These plants look like they belong in an alien jungle and will be instant conversation starters.

Best Picks:

- *Begonia maculata* – Polka-dotted leaves? It's basically wearing couture. Pictured below.

- *Ficus elastica* **'Shivereana'** – A variegated ficus that looks hand-painted.

- *Monstera* **'Peru'** – Thick, textured leaves that feel like reptile skin.

Avoid: Basic plants like peace lilies or spider plants – you need something weirder.

FINAL THOUGHTS: DON'T LET THE GARDEN CENTRE CHOOSE FOR YOU

Most people pick their first plant based on what's in stock or what an employee recommends, but that's how you end up with something that doesn't fit your space or your style.

Forget labels like 'easy' or 'beginner-friendly' and ask yourself:

- Do I actually like this plant?
- Will it survive in my home's conditions?
- Will I care enough to keep it alive?

That's the secret to choosing a plant you won't accidentally kill. Start with one that fits you and then work your way up to the divas.

Now that you've got the right plant for your space, it's time to make sure it actually stays alive. Next up? Light, because:

if your plant can't see the sky, it's already in trouble

LEVEL 2
BUDDING BOTANIST

UNDERSTANDING LIGHT REQUIREMENTS

LIGHT IS THE DIFFERENCE BETWEEN A THRIVING JUNGLE AND A SAD, LEGGY MESS.

Light isn't just important for your plants – it defines them. It dictates their growth, colour, health, even their personality.

Forget fancy soil mixes, nutrient-packed fertilisers or expensive humidity gadgets. If you don't get the light right, nothing else matters.

But here's the problem: most plant parents underestimate light.

It's easy to do, because light is deceiving. Your eyes adjust. A room might feel bright to you, but to your monstera? It's a basement with a single candle. And the worst part? Plant labels lie.

'Low light plant.' Nope.

'Thrives in indirect light.' What even is indirect light?!

'Water once a week.' What does that have to do with light?!

So, let's fix the confusion once and for all.

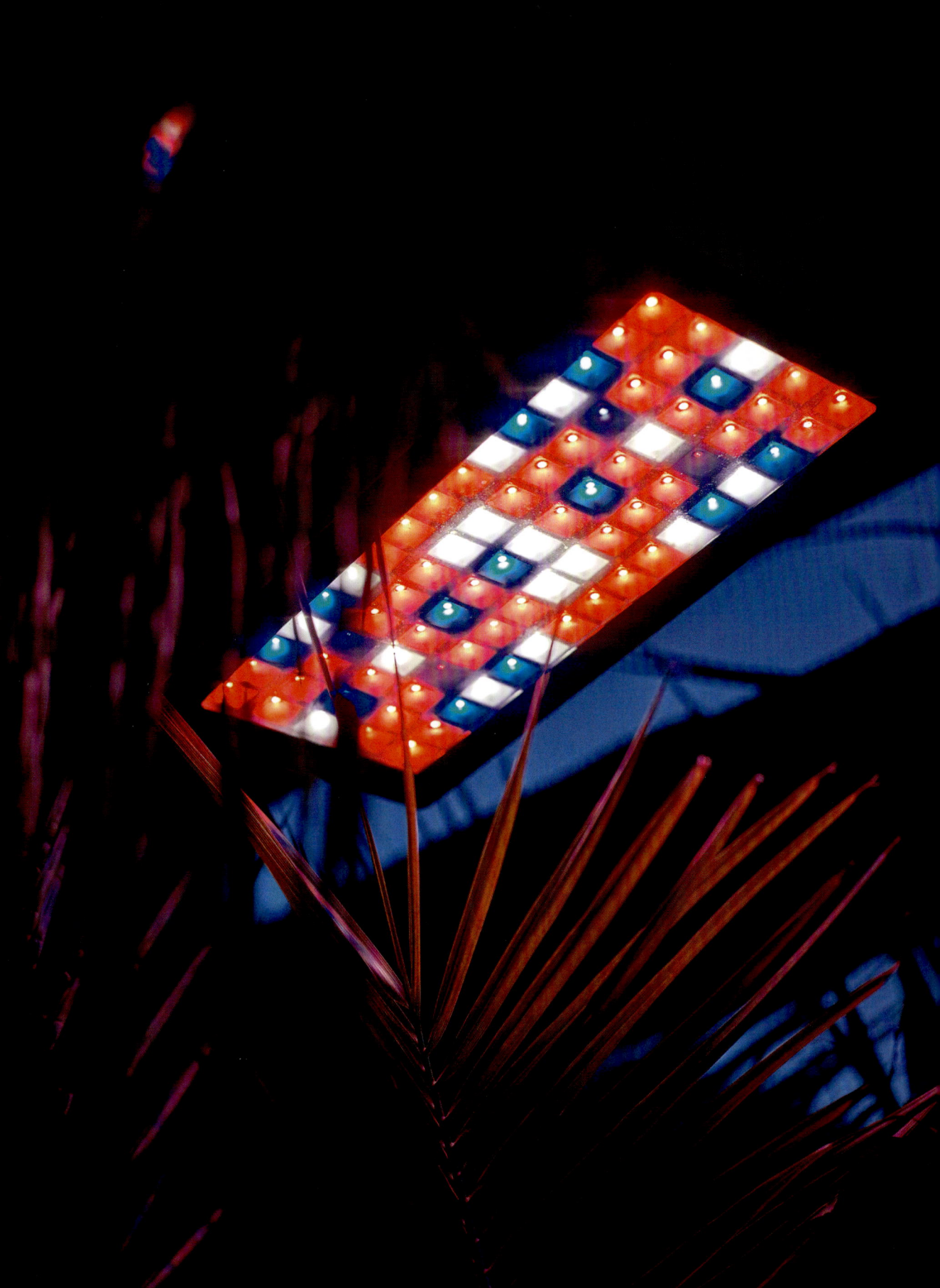

THE ULTIMATE LIGHT TEST

Forget technical terms and measuring tools. Here's how you instantly tell if your plant is getting enough light:

Get down to the plant's level. Look out the nearest window. How much sky can you see?

- **Loads of sky?** Perfect. Your plant has access to plenty of light.
- **Some sky but mostly blocked?** Decent. It'll survive, but don't expect rapid growth.
- **No sky at all?** Bad news. Your plant is light starved.

If a plant can't see the sky, it's not getting enough light to photosynthesise properly. This simple rule eliminates 90% of the confusion around indirect light.

BREAKING DOWN LIGHT LEVELS

Now that we've established that sky = light, let's talk about what different types of light actually mean inside your home.

BRIGHT, DIRECT LIGHT

Pure, unfiltered sunlight. The equivalent of lying on a beach, baking under the sun. If your plant is getting full sun for hours every day, it's in this category.

Who Loves It?

Succulents, cacti, citrus trees and sun-worshipping plants like crotons.

Signs of Too Much Direct Light:

Scorched, crispy or bleached leaves. Your monstera? It doesn't belong in direct sun – it evolved under jungle canopies.

BRIGHT, INDIRECT LIGHT

This is what most tropical plants crave – a lot of light but softened or filtered through something. Like how a monstera in the wild gets light bouncing through tree branches, but never harsh, direct sun.

Who Loves It?

Monsteras, philodendrons, calatheas, anthuriums – basically, everything that grows in jungles.

Signs of Not Enough Light:

Your plant stretches towards the window like a desperate drunk reaching for their last drink. Leaves get smaller and gaps between them get bigger.

MEDIUM LIGHT

Still fairly bright, but not strong enough to cast defined shadows. It's a few feet back from a window or a spot that only gets bright light for part of the day.

Who Loves It?

Pothos, spider plants, peace lilies and Chinese evergreens.

Signs of Not Enough Light:

Slower growth, leaves losing vibrancy and less variegation.

LOW LIGHT (AKA 'SURVIVAL MODE')

This isn't 'no light' (because no light = death), but it's dim, dull and far away from windows.

Who Can Tolerate It?

ZZ plants, snake plants, some ferns, but they won't thrive.

Signs of Light Starvation:

Barely any new growth, leaves turning yellow and looking like it's giving up on life.

REFLECTORS AND MIRRORS: BOUNCING MORE LIGHT TO YOUR PLANTS

Sometimes, you can't move your plant closer to the window. That's where reflectors and mirrors come in – they amplify and redirect light into the darker parts of your home.

Mirrors:

Place mirrors on walls opposite or beside windows to bounce light deeper into the room.

Reflective Surfaces:

Aluminium foil, white walls or reflective panels help spread light evenly, making sure no plant gets left in the shadows.

If your plants are struggling in a slightly dim area, a well placed mirror can make a HUGE difference.

Albovariegata Mint

GROW LIGHTS: THE ARTIFICIAL SUN

For some people, natural light just isn't an option. Maybe your windows are tiny. Maybe you live in the UK, where winter is just six months of grey misery.

TYPES OF GROW LIGHTS AND THEIR BENEFITS

LED (light-emitting diode) grow lights

- Most energy-efficient option.
- Full-spectrum options mimic natural sunlight.
- Low heat = no risk of burning plants.

Fluorescent grow lights (T5 and CFL bulbs)

- Great for smaller plants, seedlings and propagation.
- Less expensive than LEDs but they use more power.

HOW TO USE GROW LIGHTS THE RIGHT WAY

Positioning

- 30–60 cm (12–24 inches) above for monsteras, philodendrons and any tropical plants.
- 15–30 cm (6–12 inches) above for succulents and cacti that need stronger light.
- 10–15 cm (4–6 inches) above for seedlings and propagation stations.

Timing

- 12–16 hours per day for steady growth.
- 8 hours of darkness so plants can rest and recover.

Power consumption

- A 100W LED grow light is way cheaper to run than old fluorescent tubes.

Pro Tip: Use a timer! No one wants to manually switch lights on and off every day. Set it up, let the plants bask and relax.

THE PERSONALITY TEST: WHAT PLANTS MATCH YOUR HOME'S LIGHTING?

Not sure what to buy? Match your home's light level to the right plants:

THE SHADOW DWELLER (LOW LIGHT)

Your home has few windows or most are north-facing.

Best Picks: ZZ plant, snake plant or cast-iron plant (pictured below).

THE SUN WORSHIPPER (BRIGHT DIRECT LIGHT)

Your home is drenched in sunlight.

Best Picks: Succulents (pictured right), cacti, citrus trees or crotons.

THE INDIRECT LIGHT ENTHUSIAST (MEDIUM TO BRIGHT INDIRECT LIGHT)

Your home has decent natural light, but no direct sun.

Best Picks: Monsteras, philodendrons, calatheas or hoyas (pictured below).

THE ARTIFICIAL SUN GOD (GROW LIGHT USER)

Your home is dim, but you're committed. You're happy to set up grow lights.

Best Picks: Literally any plant, as long as you adjust the lighting! *Ficus elastica* pictured below.

FINAL THOUGHTS: LIGHT IS THE ULTIMATE CHEAT CODE

If you take one thing from this chapter, let it be this – light isn't just another care factor, it's the entire game. You can overwater a plant and still recover. You can under-fertilise and fix it later. But if your plant doesn't get the light it needs, nothing else matters.

This is why plants thrive in greenhouses but struggle in our homes. We decorate with them, place them where they 'look nice', and then wonder why they start dropping leaves like a depressed Christmas tree in January.

Plants don't care about your aesthetic.

They want light.

And now? You know the rules.

You see the sky test (page 33). You understand the difference between 'surviving' and 'thriving'. You know when to pull out the mirrors and when to bring in the grow lights.

So the next time someone asks why your monstera has leaves bigger than their head, or why your pothos is trailing like something out of *Jumanji*, you'll know the answer:

Because you didn't just 'keep a plant alive'. You gave it exactly what it needed to grow.

And THAT is the difference between a casual plant owner and a true Jungle Boss.

WATERING WISDOM

THE ART OF NOT MURDERING YOUR PLANTS WITH LOVE OR NEGLECT

Watering is supposed to be the easy part. You pour some water on the plant, it drinks, life goes on. But anyone who's ever watched a once-thriving monstera turn into a soggy, yellowing disaster knows that watering is an art. It's the single most common reason plants die, and yet, most advice out there makes it sound like something you can set a reminder for. Water once a week. Absolute nonsense.

No two plants dry out at the same rate, and no two homes have the same environment. The trick isn't to follow a schedule – it's to read the plant, the soil and the season. This chapter will teach you how to listen to your plants before they start throwing dramatic tantrums, when to water, how to water, and – most importantly – how to stop drowning or dehydrating them in the process.

SIGNS OF OVERWATERING: WHEN TOO MUCH LOVE KILLS

Overwatering is plant homicide with the best of intentions. You see a sad leaf, assume it's thirsty and before you know it, your beloved plant is sitting in a swamp of root rot. Roots need oxygen as much as they need water, and when they're constantly wet, they suffocate and rot.

The classic signs? Yellowing leaves, but not the crispy kind – the limp, 'I've given up on life' kind. Mushy stems. A damp, musty smell rising from the soil like a warning from the underworld. Fungus or mould creeping across the surface. And worst of all, no new growth – because a drowning plant stops growing long before it starts dying.

To fix it, you have to act fast. Unpot the plant, check the roots and if they're brown and mushy, cut them off – they're beyond saving. Dust the remaining healthy roots with activated charcoal to prevent further rot and repot in a well-draining mix that lets the roots breathe. If you're a chronic overwaterer, either get yourself a plant that actually wants to sit in constant moisture – like pennywort, peace lilies or semi-aquatic plants – or start bottom watering (see next page).

SIGNS OF UNDERWATERING: THE DESERT SURVIVOR'S LAMENT

On the other end of the spectrum, we have the parched, crispy, barely-holding-on plants of the world. Underwatering is less lethal than overwatering, but plants left to dry out too often will become weak and brittle, struggling to bounce back.

If your plant's leaves are curling at the edges, browning at the tips or full-on crisping up, it's screaming for water. Drooping can also be a sign, but context matters – some plants droop when they're thirsty, others when they're overwatered. The foolproof test? Stick your finger into the soil. If it's dry all the way down, give it a drink. If it's damp, leave it alone.

If your plant has been left to shrivel into a husk, don't just dump water on it and hope for the best. Extremely dry soil can become hydrophobic, meaning it repels water instead of absorbing it. If this happens, bottom watering is your best bet – set the pot in a tray of water and let it soak up moisture slowly.

WATERING TECHNIQUES: BECAUSE NOT ALL PLANTS LIKE A SHOWER

Not all watering methods are created equal. Some plants want a deep soak, others prefer a light misting (though let's be honest, misting is useless for hydration – see page 86). Here's how to match the method to the plant.

BOTTOM WATERING – THE SMART WAY TO HYDRATE

The plant sits in a tray of water and absorbs moisture through the drainage holes. This method prevents overwatering, encourages deep root growth and stops water from sitting on the leaves (especially good for plants prone to fungal issues). Best for fussy plants like calatheas, fittonias and peperomias.

DEEP WATERING – A PROPER DRINK, NOT JUST A SIP

The goal is to soak the soil thoroughly until water runs out of the drainage holes of the pots. This ensures the entire root system gets moisture, not just the top layer of soil. Best for monsteras, philodendrons and large plants in chunky soil mixes.

SOAKING – WHEN A PLANT NEEDS EMERGENCY HYDRATION

If the soil has become completely dry and water runs right through without soaking in, submerge the pot in a basin of water and let it sit for 20–30 minutes. This forces hydration back into the soil. Ideal for severely dehydrated plants or those in terracotta pots.

WATER QUALITY: WHAT'S REALLY IN YOUR TAP WATER?

Not all water is the same, and some plants are incredibly picky. Tap water is usually fine for most plants, but if you keep seeing brown leaf tips on your calatheas or peace lilies, your water might be the culprit. High levels of chlorine, fluoride or hard minerals can build up in the soil over time, stressing plants out.

Rainwater is the gold standard – free of chemicals and packed with trace minerals that plants love. Distilled water is also a good option, though it lacks those minerals, so occasional fertilising is necessary. If you must use tap water, let it sit for 24 hours before watering to allow chlorine to evaporate.

THE SEASONAL SHIFT: WHY YOUR WATERING ROUTINE NEEDS TO ADAPT

Plants don't need the same amount of water all year round. Growth slows in autumn and winter, meaning less water is needed. Overwatering a dormant plant is one of the quickest ways to kill it – if it's not actively growing, it's not drinking as much.

But what if your home is warm and your heating is on? Dry indoor air can trick you into thinking your plant needs more water when it actually needs more humidity. If your plant is near a radiator, move it or increase humidity with a pebble tray or humidifier. If you're using grow lights (see page 36), your plants might keep growing through winter, meaning they'll still need a regular watering schedule.

Summer is the opposite – higher temperatures and increased evaporation mean you'll be watering more often. But don't assume – always check the soil first.

HUMIDITY HACKS: BECAUSE SOME PLANTS WANT TO LIVE IN A STEAM ROOM

If you own tropical plants, watering alone isn't enough – humidity is just as important. Dry air can cause leaves to crisp up no matter how perfectly you're watering. If your ferns, anthuriums or alocasias are suffering, humidity (or lack of it) is likely the issue.

Pebble trays help, but the real MVP is a humidifier (see page 86). If you're serious about keeping humidity-loving plants happy, just get one. Your plants (and your skin) will thank you.

THE PERSONALITY TEST: WHICH WATERING TYPE ARE YOU?

THE SERIAL DROWNER

You love your plants too much and can't resist watering them daily. Get yourself a pennywort (pictured right) or if you don't like semi-aquatic plants, a peace lily!

THE BALANCED HYDRATOR

You check the soil before watering, understand seasonal shifts and never panic-water. Philodendrons, monsteras and pothos (pictured above) will thrive in your care.

THE FORGETFUL DESERT WANDERER

You mean well, but life gets in the way and suddenly it's been 3 weeks since your plants saw water. Stick to cacti, snake plants (pictured below) and ZZ plants.

THE 'I'LL WATER WHEN I FEEL LIKE IT' TYPE

You're unpredictable, so you need plants that don't mind inconsistency. Pothos, spider plants and dracaenas (pictured to the right) are perfect for your 'water when you remember' approach.

**FINAL THOUGHTS:
WATERING IS AN ART, NOT A SCHEDULE**

Forget everything you've been told about watering once a week. Listen to your plants. Stick your finger into the soil. Learn the weight of your pot when it's dry versus when it's freshly watered. Your plants don't want a rigid schedule – they want you to pay attention.

Master this, and watering will stop being a guessing game. It'll be instinct. And your plants? They'll thrive like never before.

Forget everything you've been told about watering once a week

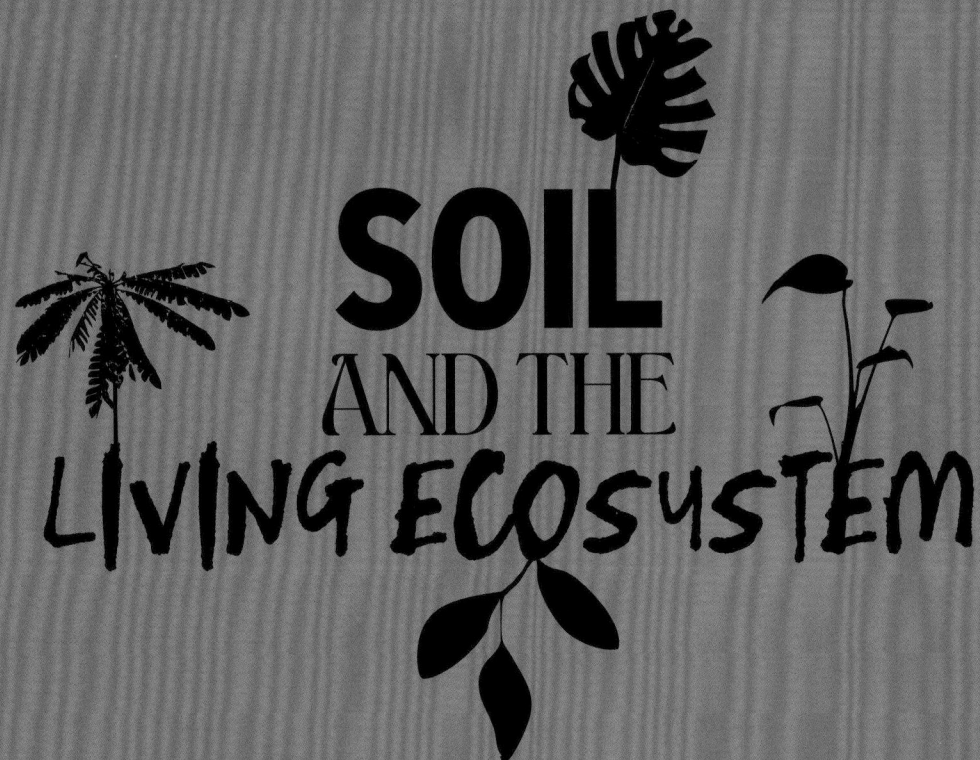

SOIL AND THE LIVING ECOSYSTEM

WHERE LIFE BEGINS

Soil. It's where everything starts. It's the difference between a plant that thrives and one that limps along, forever teetering on the edge of death. It's not just dirt; it's the foundation, the pantry, the oxygen supplier, the water reservoir, the support system. It's an entire ecosystem, alive with activity, constantly shifting and evolving beneath the surface.

And yet, most people treat soil as an afterthought. They grab a bag of whatever's cheapest, stuff it in a pot, plant something in it and then wonder why their new monstera starts looking like it's seen some things. But the truth is, if your soil is wrong, everything is wrong. No amount of watering schedules, fertilisers or grow lights can save a plant whose roots are suffocating in compacted, lifeless muck.

So, let's get this right. Let's build a soil mix that actually works, one that provides structure, nutrients, airflow and moisture balance – the kind of mix that turns plant care from a constant battle into something effortless.

THE UNDERGROUND JUNGLE: A WORLD IN MOTION

Take a moment to think about what's happening beneath the surface of a thriving plant. Its roots aren't just sitting there passively waiting for you to water them – they're stretching, reaching, exploring. They're interacting with bacteria and fungi, exchanging nutrients, forming relationships with microorganisms that help break down organic matter into plant food.

Healthy soil is alive, teeming with tiny organisms that make nutrients available, fight off pathogens and maintain balance. But bagged potting soil? That stuff is dead. Sterilised, stripped of life, often packed with peat that compacts over time, suffocating roots instead of supporting them. If you want plants that thrive, you need to create soil that breathes, moves and sustains itself.

Let's talk ingredients.

CRAFTING THE PERFECT SOIL MIX

A good soil mix needs four things:

- **Structure** – To give roots something to anchor to while allowing airflow.
- **Aeration** – Because roots need oxygen just as much as they need water.
- **Moisture control** – Enough to keep plants hydrated but never waterlogged.
- **Nutrients** – Because a plant can't survive on water alone.

The way I mix my soil depends on the plant, but my base ingredients are always the same:

- **Compost** – The organic backbone, packed with nutrients and microbial life.
- **Worm castings** – The single best natural fertiliser, full of plant-available nutrients.
- **Perlite** – The aeration hero, keeping soil light and fluffy.
- **Pine bark** – Adds structure and encourages beneficial fungi.
- **Sphagnum moss** – Holds moisture without getting soggy.
- **LECA balls** – Improves drainage and creates air pockets.
- **Horticultural grit** – Adds weight and drainage without compacting.

And if I'm feeling fancy (or if I have them on hand), I'll throw in:

- **Sand** – Helps with drainage and adds texture.
- **Vermiculite** – Holds onto moisture while keeping soil airy.
- **Activated charcoal** – Absorbs impurities and prevents excess moisture buildup.

These ingredients create a soil that breathes, providing the perfect balance between water retention and drainage.

SOIL RECIPES

The Golden Rule of Soil Testing

Here's how you know if your soil mix is actually right: grab a handful, squeeze it tightly in your fist and then release it.

- If it crumbles apart naturally, you've nailed it – your mix has the perfect amount of aeration and drainage.
- If it sticks together in a dense, compacted clump, it's too heavy – you need more perlite, pine bark or grit to keep things light.

This one simple trick will save you from suffocating your plant's roots and ensure you've got a soil mix that breathes.

CLEARING UP THE CHARCOAL CONFUSION

A lot of people hear that charcoal 'prevents fungal growth' and immediately assume it's a bad idea in a living soil mix (see page 61 to learn about living soil). Here's the truth: charcoal absorbs excess moisture and toxins, but it doesn't kill off the good guys.

Beneficial fungi – the kind that break down organic matter and transport nutrients – are essential to healthy soil. Charcoal only helps regulate moisture levels, preventing conditions where harmful fungi (the root rot-causing kind) take over. So, when used in small amounts, it actually helps maintain the balance of the ecosystem.

THE EVERYDAY MIX (FOR MOST HOUSEPLANTS AND AROIDS)

- **40% Compost** – The main nutrient base, full of life.
- **15% Worm castings** – Supercharges the mix with slow-release nutrition.
- **15% Perlite** – Keeps the soil aerated, preventing compaction.
- **15% Pine bark** – Adds structure and promotes microbial activity.
- **10% Sphagnum moss** – Holds moisture without drowning roots.
- **5% LECA balls and horticultural grit** – Improves drainage and keeps the mix from compacting.

THE PERSONALITY TEST: WHAT'S YOUR SOIL STYLE?

THE SUPER CHUNKY JUNGLE MIX (FOR ORCHIDS AND ANTHURIUMS)

You love big, dramatic foliage with thick, wild roots. Your plants hate wet, compact soil and need a mix so airy you could blow through it. This is next-level chunkiness, designed for plants that naturally cling to tree trunks and thrive in humid air, not dense soil.

If You Love These Plants, This Mix Is for You:

- **Anthuriums** – *A. clarinervium, A. warocqueanum, A. crystallinum*
- **Orchids** – *Phalaenopsis, Oncidium*

Your Soil Base:

- **40% Pine bark** – Mimics tree bark, giving roots space to breathe.
- **20% Perlite** – Keeps it light and aerated.
- **15% Sphagnum moss** – Holds just enough moisture without getting soggy.
- **10% Worm castings** – Adds nutrients in an organic, slow-release form.
- **10% LECA balls** – Prevents compaction and enhances drainage.
- **5% Compost** – Just a touch of organic matter for a nutrient boost.

This mix mimics the way anthuriums and orchids grow in the wild – plenty of airflow, moisture control and no heavy soil to suffocate roots.

Pine bark

Worm castings

Perlite

THE JUNGLE CLIMBER MIX (FOR MONSTERA, PHILODENDRON, SYNGONIUM, RHAPHIDOPHORA AND EPIPREMNUM)

You love lush, vining plants with dramatic aerial roots that climb anything in sight. These plants don't want super-chunky soil, but they need enough drainage to prevent rot. They love a balanced mix that's not too dense, not too airy – just right.

If You Love These Plants, This Mix Is for You:

- **Monstera** – *deliciosa*, 'Albo', 'Peru'
- **Philodendrons** – 'Micans', 'Pink Princess', *P. verrucosum*
- **Syngoniums** – 'Mojito', 'Albo', 'Pink Splash'
- **Rhaphidophoras** – *R. tetrasperma*, *R. decursiva*
- **Epipremnum** – *Epipremnum aureum*, 'Cebu Blue', 'Neon'

Your Soil Base:

- **30% Pine bark** – Keeps structure and aeration balanced.
- **25% Compost** – Provides slow-release nutrients.
- **20% Perlite** – Prevents waterlogging.
- **10% Worm castings** – Feeds the plant naturally.
- **10% LECA balls** – Adds aeration and prevents compaction.
- **5% Horticultural grit** – Enhances drainage.

This mix mimics the loose, rich, well-draining forest floors these plants naturally thrive in. It holds onto moisture but never stays soggy, making it perfect for fast growing, trailing and climbing jungle plants.

LECA balls

Compost

THE MOISTURE LOVER'S DREAM MIX (FOR CALATHEAS, PEACE LILIES, ALOCASIAS AND FERNS)

You love dramatic foliage and plants that demand humidity and regular watering. These plants hate drying out completely but still need some drainage to prevent rot. They want moisture, but with a bit of breathing room.

If You Love These Plants, This Mix Is for You:

- **Calatheas** – *Calathea orbifolia*, *C.* 'Medallion', *C.* 'Fusion White'
- **Peace lilies** – *Spathiphyllum* 'Sensation'
- **Alocasias** – *Alocasia × amazonica* 'Polly', *A.* 'Dragon Scale', *A.* 'Frydek'
- **Ferns** – Boston fern, maidenhair, staghorn

Your Soil Base:

- **35% Compost** – Holds moisture and feeds plants.
- **20% Sphagnum moss** – Helps retain water for longer hydration.
- **20% Vermiculite** – Absorbs water and releases it slowly.
- **10% Worm castings** – Keeps the nutrients flowing.
- **10% Perlite** – Ensures some airflow for root health.
- **5% Activated charcoal** – Prevents mould, keeps the mix fresh.

This mix is moisture-retentive but breathable – the sweet spot for water-loving tropicals that wilt if they dry out. If you're growing peace lilies, increase the compost for even more water retention.

Vermiculite

Sphagnum moss

Activated charcoal

THE DESERT SURVIVOR MIX (FOR CACTI AND SUCCULENTS)

You love tough, drought-loving plants that prefer neglect over too much attention. These plants store water in their leaves and hate sitting in damp soil. If the mix stays wet for too long, it's game over.

If You Love These Plants, This Mix Is for You:

- **Cacti** – Golden barrel, prickly pear, bunny ear
- **Succulents** – Jade plant, aloe vera, echeveria
- **Sansevieria (snake plants)** – *laurentii*, 'Moonshine', *Sansevieria masoniana*
- **Agaves and yuccas** – *Agave americana*, *Yucca rostrata*

Your Soil Base:

- **35% Horticultural grit** – Keeps soil dry and airy.
- **25% Sand** – Ensures rapid drainage.
- **20% Perlite** – Further enhances the oxygen flow.
- **10% Compost** – A tiny amount for slow-release nutrients.
- **5% Worm castings** – Provides essential minerals.
- **5% Activated charcoal** – Prevents bacterial growth.

This mix mimics arid, rocky environments, ensuring that water drains quickly while still giving plants the essential nutrients they need.

Horticultural grit

Sand

FINAL THOUGHTS: SOIL IS THE UNSUNG HERO OF PLANT CARE

People talk endlessly about watering schedules and light conditions, but soil is what really makes or breaks a plant's health. Get the mix right, and your plants will thrive with minimal fuss. Get it wrong, and you'll be battling root rot, dehydration and nutrient deficiencies from day one.

So – which mix suits your jungle? Are you the Super Chunky Orchid and Anthurium Lover, the Jungle Climber Enthusiast, the Moisture Addict or the Desert Survivor?

Whichever one you are, you now have the perfect formula to match your plants to the soil they actually want to live in.

LEVEL 3
PLANT GUARDIAN

NUTRIENT KNOW-HOW

Just like you need a good meal to keep going, your plants need proper nutrition to thrive. The nutrients in the soil provide the fuel for growth, but over time they get used up, especially if your plant is in a pot where fresh soil isn't constantly being replenished. That's where fertilisers come in – they're like plant vitamins that help replenish the nutrients your plants need to stay strong, green and healthy.

But here's the catch: too much fertiliser can be just as harmful as too little. In this chapter, we'll break down the essentials of plant nutrition, how to choose the right fertilisers and when and how to feed your plants for the best results.

Philodendron giganteum

THE BIG THREE: N-P-K AND WHAT IT MEANS

You've probably noticed fertiliser labels with three numbers – this is the N-P-K ratio, which stands for Nitrogen (N), Phosphorus (P), and Potassium (K). These are the three major nutrients your plant needs to grow, and each one plays a specific role:

- **Nitrogen (N)** – Helps with leaf growth and gives your plants that lush, green look. This is the nutrient responsible for healthy, vigorous foliage.

- **Phosphorus (P)** – Promotes strong root development and is key for flowering and fruiting. If you want beautiful blooms or tasty fruit, phosphorus is your plant's best friend.

- **Potassium (K)** – Boosts overall plant health, helping plants resist disease and withstand stress, like drought or cold.

Most fertilisers will list these three numbers on the packaging (e.g. 10-10-10 or 5-10-5). Each plant has different nutrient needs, so getting the balance right is important.

MACRO VS. MICRO: THE FULL NUTRIENT PICTURE

While N-P-K are the big three, they aren't the only nutrients your plant needs. Plants also require secondary nutrients (like calcium, magnesium and sulphur) and micronutrients (like iron, zinc and manganese) to stay healthy.

- **Calcium** – Helps build strong cell walls, giving plants structure and preventing problems like blossom end rot in fruiting plants.

- **Magnesium** – Essential for photosynthesis (that magic process that helps plants turn light into energy).

- **Iron** – Helps with chlorophyll production, keeping your plants green and healthy.

These nutrients might not get as much attention, but they play an important role in keeping your plants in top shape.

CHOOSING THE RIGHT FERTILISER: TAILORED NUTRITION FOR YOUR PLANTS

With so many fertilisers on the market, it can feel overwhelming to pick the right one. But once you understand what your plants need, it's easier to make an informed choice. Here are the main types of fertilisers:

- **Balanced fertilisers** – A safe bet for general houseplants, offering an even N-P-K ratio (e.g. 10-10-10).

- **High-nitrogen fertilisers** – Perfect for leafy plants like monstera, ferns or calatheas (e.g. 20-10-10).

- **High-phosphorus fertilisers** – Essential for flowering and fruiting plants (e.g. 5-10-5 for peace lilies, citrus trees, etc.).

- **Organic fertilisers** – Compost, worm castings or fish emulsion provide a natural, slow-release nutrient boost.

Philodendron hederaceum var. hederaceum

FEEDING SCHEDULES: WHEN AND HOW OFTEN TO FERTILISE

Plants don't need to be fed every day – just like you wouldn't take vitamins with every meal. The key to successful fertilising is getting the timing and frequency right:

- **Growing season (spring and summer)** – Every 2–4 weeks, depending on the plant's needs.
- **Dormant season (autumn and winter)** – Reduce feeding or stop entirely if growth slows.
- **Artificially lit plants** – If your plants are growing under grow lights, they might not experience dormancy and may still need regular feeding.

In my home, where about 70% of my plant care is in an artificial environment, I use an extremely weak feed with every watering (about every 3–4 weeks). This keeps feeding balanced and prevents nutrient overload.

SIGNS OF OVER-FERTILISATION: DON'T BURN YOUR PLANTS

Fertilisers are like vitamins – too much can cause more harm than good. Over-fertilising can lead to fertiliser burn, where the salts in the fertiliser build up and damage the plant's roots. Signs of over-fertilisation include:

- **Brown or crispy leaf edges** – Salt buildup damaging the roots.
- **Slow or stunted growth** – Too much fertiliser can actually stress the plant out.
- **White crust on the soil surface** – Excess fertiliser salts building up in the soil.

If you suspect you've over-fertilised, flush the soil with water to wash away excess nutrients.

LIVING SOIL: THE FERTILISER-FREE ALTERNATIVE

Now, what if I told you that you might not need fertiliser at all? If you're using a living soil mix – which includes compost, worm castings and a rich microbial ecosystem – your plants may already be getting a steady supply of nutrients without the need for synthetic feeds. Living soil acts as a self-sustaining ecosystem where beneficial microorganisms continuously break down organic matter into plant-available nutrients, providing a slow-release, balanced diet for your plants.

If you build a thriving soil microbiome, your plants can feed themselves naturally over time, without the risk of over-fertilising.

Monstera pinnatipartita

THE PERSONALITY TEST: FERTILISER FANS

Every plant parent has a unique approach to feeding, so let's match you with the plants that'll thrive with your style of nutrient care:

THE BALANCED FEEDER

Love monsteras, pothos or philodendrons? A well-rounded, general-purpose fertiliser is your best bet. These classic houseplants will thrive with a balanced N-P-K ratio and show steady growth without needing anything too specialised.

THE ORGANIC ENTHUSIAST

Peace lilies, rubber plants or dracaenas? These plants prefer a natural, slow-release feed. They'll love compost, worm castings and organic liquid feeds that build soil health.

THE HIGH-PROTEIN PROVIDER

If you're into palms, spider plants or Boston ferns, you're a nitrogen-lover. These plants demand a high-nitrogen fertiliser to stay lush and full.

THE LIVING SOIL BELIEVER

If you're into monsteras, philodendrons or pothos but want to avoid synthetic fertilisers altogether, living soil is the way forward. With worm castings, compost and beneficial microbes, you can create a naturally self-sustaining system – no need for bottled feeds.

THE BLOOM BOOSTER

If you're all about fruiting and flowering plants like African violets, hibiscus or citrus trees, you need a high-phosphorus fertiliser to boost blooming and root strength.

FINAL THOUGHTS: FERTILISING

Fertilising your plants is like giving them the fuel they need to thrive – but it's all about balance. By understanding the basics of N-P-K, choosing the right fertiliser (or building nutrient-rich living soil) and following a feeding schedule that fits your plant's needs, you'll be able to keep your plants healthy, vibrant and full of life.

Remember, every plant is different, so don't be afraid to experiment and find what works best for your leafy friends. Whether you're using organic fertilisers, synthetic feeds or embracing the wonders of living soil, the goal is to build a thriving, self-sustaining environment where plants flourish naturally.

PEST PATROL

Welcome to the ugly side of houseplant care – the part they don't put on the glossy Instagram posts. Pests. If you've got plants, you've got pests. It's just a matter of when you notice them.

And I'll tell you now: you will never be completely pest-free. The trick isn't to aim for an impossible utopia where not a single critter exists – it's to manage them, keep their numbers low and prevent them from turning your monstera into an all-you-can-eat buffet.

Let's get one thing straight: pests aren't just an attack on your plants. They're an attack on you. Your pride, your patience, your willingness to keep going when yet another leaf turns into a lace doily overnight. But fear not – we're going to break this down, figure out exactly who the enemy is and talk about how to fight back without losing your sanity.

> *Pests aren't just an attack on your plants. They're an attack on you.*

MEET THE BASTARDS: THE MOST COMMON HOUSEPLANT PESTS

SPIDER MITES — THE INVISIBLE TERRORISTS

These microscopic sap-sucking nightmares are nearly impossible to spot until the damage is done. One day your plant is fine; the next, the leaves look like they've been dusted with ash, curling and speckled, with fine, silky webs on the undersides. They thrive in dry conditions, multiply at a ridiculous rate and can absolutely demolish an entire plant collection before you even realise they're there.

How to Spot Them: Speckled, faded, curling leaves and those sneaky little webs.

THRIPS — THE GRIM REAPERS

Thrips don't nibble on plants – they suck the life force out of them. These elongated, black or tan insects scrape away the surface of leaves, leaving behind silvery, damaged tissue. They spread like wildfire and are absolute hell to get rid of. If spider mites are the terrorists of the plant world, thrips are the bloody grim reapers.

How to Spot Them: Silvery streaks, distorted growth and tiny, fast-moving black specks on your leaves.

MEALYBUGS — FLUFFY WHITE WANKERS

These little cottony freeloaders are the cockroaches of the plant world – they get everywhere, multiply like mad and refuse to die. They love hiding in leaf joints and crevices, slowly draining the life from your plant while leaving behind a sticky, sugary mess that attracts mould and more pests.

How to Spot Them: White, fluffy, waxy blobs clustered at the base of leaves or along stems.

APHIDS — THE LITTLE GREEN LEECHES

Aphids are tiny, pear-shaped and usually green (but sometimes black or yellow). They camp out on new growth, sucking the juices out and distorting leaves. They also poop out sugary honeydew, which attracts even more issues. Annoying? Yes. Beatable? Absolutely.

How to Spot Them: Distorted new growth, sticky residue on plants and clusters of tiny, soft-bodied insects.

SCALE — THE ARMOURED PESTS

Scale insects don't even look like insects. They look like hard, brown or tan bumps stuck to stems and leaves. They don't move, they don't crawl, they just sit there like leeches, sucking the life out of your plants and refusing to budge.

How to Spot Them: Hard, flat bumps that don't scrape off easily.

FUNGUS GNATS — THE ANNOYING FREELOADERS

Unlike other pests, fungus gnats don't attack your leaves – they lay eggs in your soil, and their larvae feast on your plant's roots. The adults are tiny black flies that hover around like they own the place.

How to Spot Them: Tiny black flies buzzing around the soil and stunted growth.

The Gnat Rant: Too many people ask me about fungus gnats. Those tiny, relentless specks of irritation that hover around your plants and make you question your life choices when one decides to kamikaze straight into your coffee. Let's clear up the confusion: the adults don't harm your plants at all. They don't bite, they don't chew, they don't suck – they just exist to be annoying. The reason they seem to be launching themselves at your face? They're attracted to the carbon dioxide in your breath. Congratulations, you're officially the hottest club in town for fungus gnats.

The real issue comes from their larvae, which hatch in your soil and can munch on plant roots if you've got a full-blown infestation. But honestly? If you've reached that point, your soil is staying way too wet, and you need to rethink your watering habits.

Want to get rid of them? Step one: fix your soil. They thrive in damp, compacted, consistently moist soil – so if you keep drowning your plants, you're basically rolling out the red carpet for them. Use a chunky, well draining mix, and let the top inch or two of soil dry out between waterings. If the larvae don't have moisture to survive, they die.

If you're already dealing with an infestation, try bottom-watering instead of top-watering for a while – this stops them from laying eggs in the first place. Sticky traps will catch the adults (which is weirdly satisfying), but the real fix is drying out your soil and getting your watering routine right. You can also use nematodes (see below).

Fungus gnats are not a sign you're a bad plant parent – just an overenthusiastic waterer. Dry things out, adjust your soil mix and watch them disappear like an ex who finally takes the hint.

THE WAR PLAN: HOW TO FIGHT BACK

STEP 1: THE SHOCK AND AWE TREATMENT – MY GO-TO ATTACK PLAN

Here's my personal pest control routine – tested in battle and proven effective. When I see pests, I don't mess about:

1. **Hose the plant down** – If I can move it, I give it a high-pressure shower to physically remove as many pests as possible. (If I can't move it, I just squash them on sight.)
2. **Neem oil and horticultural soap spray** – This is my weapon of choice. Neem oil disrupts the pests' hormonal systems (so they forget how to eat, mate and generally exist), while a few drops of washing-up liquid (yes, Fairy Liquid works) break down their protective layers and suffocate them.
3. **Twice-weekly sprays** – Pest control is not a one-time job. I spray down my plants twice a week to make sure I get every generation of pests as they hatch.

STEP 2: BIOLOGICAL WARFARE – LET NATURE HANDLE IT

If you prefer a hands-off approach, you can unleash an army of predator insects. Just be warned: these solutions take time.

- **Predator mites** – Eat spider mites for breakfast.
- **Ladybugs** – Love aphids (but are useless indoors unless you have a big infestation).
- **Nematodes** – Microscopic worms that attack fungus gnat larvae in the soil.

If you're squeamish about introducing more bugs, stick to my neem oil routine.

STEP 3: CHEMICAL WARFARE – WHEN YOU NEED THE BIG GUNS

Sometimes, bugs won't take the hint. If you've hosed, sprayed, prayed, released an insect army, and they're still partying on your plant like it's 1999, it might be time to bring in synthetics.

Systemic pesticides are absorbed into the plant itself, meaning when a pest bites into it, they get a nasty surprise and drop dead shortly after. It's a full-body defence system, like vaccinating your plant with venom.

You'll usually find these under names like imidacloprid or acetamiprid, sold in soil drenches or sprays. But before you go full Rambo, keep this in mind:

- They can harm beneficial insects, especially if you're also using biological methods (don't mix your armies).
- Always read the label and stick to houseplant-safe options.
- Don't go overboard – these are for serious infestations, not a single aphid with a death wish. Think of this like calling in air support. Effective, but not for everyday skirmishes.

STEP 4: THE REALITY CHECK – LIVING WITH PESTS

Look, you will never be 100% pest-free. There will always be a few lurking around, waiting for their moment. The key is to keep them under control, not to drive yourself insane trying to eliminate every last one.

If you've tried everything and the battle is stressing you out more than the plant is bringing you joy, do yourself a favour: ditch the plant. No shame in it. If you're losing sleep over a constant infestation, cut your losses and move on.

THE PERSONALITY TEST: PEST-PROOF PLANTS

THE FORT KNOX PLANT — BUILT FOR WAR

Hate dealing with pests? Stick to snake plants, ZZ plants and cast-iron plants. These guys are as close to pest-proof as it gets.

THE BEAUTIFUL DISASTER — HIGH-MAINTENANCE DRAMA QUEEN

Love a challenge? Alocasias, calatheas and maidenhair ferns attract pests like a free buffet — but if you win the battle, they'll reward you with their stunning foliage.

THE NATURAL DEFENDER — SMELLS LIKE VICTORY

If you like a bit of natural protection, go for rosemary, lavender or mint — these plants have built-in pest-repelling properties.

THE LUSH SURVIVOR — PEST-TOLERANT BEAUTY

Monsteras, philodendrons and rubber trees are tough enough to take a few bites and keep growing strong.

FINAL THOUGHTS: KNOW WHEN TO FIGHT AND WHEN TO LET GO

Pests are inevitable, but they don't have to ruin your plant journey. Learn how to manage them, stay consistent with treatment and know when to walk away from a battle that's not worth fighting.

At the end of the day, your plants should be a source of joy, not stress. Keep an eye out, take action early and remember – you're the boss, not the bugs.

Remember you're the boss, not the bugs

PROPAGATION
GROWING YOUR COLLECTION FOR FREE

Imagine if every time you trimmed your hair, the cuttings sprouted into full-grown clones of yourself. Creepy? Yes. Useful? Absolutely. That's exactly what propagation is – a plant's superpower to regenerate and multiply – and if you master it, you'll never have to buy another plant again (unless you're a hopeless addict, in which case, same).

Propagation isn't just a neat trick; it's power. It's the closest thing to playing god in your indoor jungle. You can bend nature to your will, create clones and expand your empire – all from a single cutting. But let's get something straight: it's not always instant success. Sometimes, you end up staring at a pathetic lump of stem for weeks before anything happens. Sometimes, it rots. Sometimes, it ghosts you completely.

That's why propagation isn't just a skill; it's an art. An art of patience, experimentation and, let's be honest, a little blind faith. But once you get the hang of it? You'll be unstoppable.

THE PROPAGATION TRAP: THE MYTH OF INSTANT SUCCESS

There's a huge misconception about propagation – people think it's as easy as sticking a cutting in water and watching roots explode overnight. Wrong. Some plants root quickly, while others take their sweet, unbothered time, testing your patience like a houseguest who overstays their welcome.

The truth? Propagation is a waiting game. Some cuttings will root in days, some in weeks, some in months. Some plants just refuse – I'm looking at you, stubborn *Monstera obliqua*. The secret is knowing what method suits which plant and what level of commitment you're willing to put in.

CUTTING TO THE CHASE: WHERE AND HOW TO CUT

Not all cuttings are created equal. If you're going in blind, you might as well be hacking at your plant with a butter knife. Here's what you need to know:

STEM CUTTINGS

For vining plants like pothos, philodendrons and monsteras, you want a cutting with at least one node (that little bump on the stem where roots and leaves sprout). Cut just below the node to give the plant a fresh spot to root from. Remove lower leaves so they don't rot in water or soil.

LEAF CUTTINGS

Some plants, like snake plants and succulents, can grow an entirely new plant from a single leaf. But don't just chuck it on the soil and hope for the best – succulents need to callus over (when a plant's cut surface dries and hardens to protect against rot and infection before new growth can emerge) first before being placed on slightly moist soil. Meanwhile, snake plant cuttings can be stuck into soil or water and will eventually sprout tiny pups.

DIVISION

For plants that grow in clumps (such as peace lilies, ferns, ZZ plants), the best method is simply pulling them apart like tangled headphones. Gently separate them at the roots, ensuring each section has a decent root system before repotting.

AIR LAYERING

For bigger plants like fiddle-leaf figs and rubber plants, air layering is like performing surgery – but with a guaranteed success rate. Make a small cut on a mature stem, wrap the wound in moist sphagnum moss and cover it with plastic wrap. In 4–8 weeks, roots will form and you can snip your new baby free.

DO CUTTINGS NEED LIGHT? HOW LONG DOES THIS TAKE?

Yes, absolutely. Cuttings still need light to photosynthesise (even if they don't have roots yet). They thrive in bright, indirect light – too much direct sun and they'll fry; too little and they'll sulk. Rooting times vary:

- **Fast rooters** – Like pothos and philodendrons: 1–3 weeks.
- **Medium rooters** – Like monsteras and snake plants: 4–6 weeks.
- **Slowcoaches** – Like fiddle-leaf figs: 8+ weeks (if they're feeling generous).

FISH TANK PROPAGATION AND THE MAGIC OF FISH POOP

Fish tanks are a propagation goldmine. If you've got a freshwater tank, you already have:

Nutrient-rich water – Full of fish waste = natural fertiliser.

Oxygenated water – From air stones or filters, helping cuttings root faster.

Stable warmth – Which tropical plants love.

Just clip your cuttings and let them float near the surface for anywhere between two weeks to a month and a half, depending on the plant (it's best to wait until secondary roots appear – the thinner roots that branch off the initial main root – as they improve nutrient uptake and help the plant transition more successfully when moved to soil or another medium).

Bonus: fish tank water is amazing for watering your plants – zero chemicals, packed with nitrates and it supercharges growth.

THE POWER OF CHODES: EVEN THE SMALLEST STEMS HAVE POTENTIAL

Some of the most underrated propagations come from stem chunks without leaves. I call them chodes – because they're short, stubby and don't look like much, but boy do they have potential. As long as they've got a node, they can sprout. Keep them humid, warm and give them time – they'll surprise you.

MY PREFERRED PROPAGATION BOX RECIPE

The propagation box is like a luxury spa retreat for cuttings – high humidity, aeration and the perfect environment to encourage roots. Here's how I set up mine:

1. **First layer: perlite** – For drainage, because no one likes wet feet.

2. **Second layer: sphagnum moss** – Acts as a moisture reservoir but doesn't drown the cuttings.

3. **Third layer: the magic mix** –

   - 1 part compost – slow-release nutrients for when roots develop.
   - 1 part perlite – prevents soil from compacting.
   - 1 part vermiculite – holds just enough moisture without causing rot.
   - ½ part activated charcoal – keeps things fresh but doesn't kill beneficial fungi.
   - ½ part worm castings – boosts microbial life and gives cuttings the best start.
   - 1 part pine bark – adds structure and aeration.

4. **Fourth layer: sphagnum moss** – Keeps it fluffy – acts as a moisture reservoir, cushioning the cuttings in place.

If you prefer a more controlled approach, LECA or moss propagation can help manage moisture levels precisely. Label your cuttings unless you like playing botanical roulette.

THE PERSONALITY TEST: WHAT'S YOUR PROPAGATION STYLE?

THE WATER WATCHER

Love to see roots develop daily? Try pothos, philodendrons and monsteras – they root fast and visibly in water.

THE EXPERIMENTAL PROPAGATOR

Want a challenge? Air layer a fiddle-leaf fig or rubber plant for high success rates.

THE SUCCULENT GROWER

Patient and playing the long game? Jade plants, snake plants and echeveria root slowly but surely.

THE MULTI-PLANT MANIAC

Want instant gratification? Peace lilies, bird of paradise and ZZ plants divide beautifully.

FINAL THOUGHTS: PROPAGATION IS MAGIC – BUT ALSO CHAOS

Pruning and propagation aren't just plant care – they're next-level jungle mastery. Sure, sometimes cuttings rot. Sometimes you wait weeks with no results. Sometimes you forget about them entirely and months later – boom, new plant.

But the magic of propagation is that it always offers a second chance. If one method fails, try another. If one chode refuses to root, another will rise to the challenge.

So go forth, multiply your jungle and revel in the chaos – because this is how plant parents become plant gods.

This is how plant parents become plant gods

LEVEL 4
ADVANCED CULTIVATOR

HUMIDITY
AND AIR QUALITY
THE UNSEEN LIFELINE OF YOUR JUNGLE

Imagine trying to survive in the desert when you're built for the rainforest. That's exactly what happens to your plants when they don't get the humidity they need.

You might not see humidity, but your plants? They feel every single drop – or lack of it. And if you get it wrong, they'll let you know with crisped-up edges, curled leaves and a general air of resentment, like a houseplant version of someone giving you the silent treatment.

Humidity isn't just a fancy extra; for some plants, it's a lifeline. It dictates how well they absorb water, how efficiently they photosynthesise and, ultimately, whether they thrive or slowly wither into an expensive pile of compost. So, let's get this straight – understanding and controlling humidity is not optional if you want that lush, thriving jungle look.

HUMIDITY 101: WHAT IT ACTUALLY DOES

Humidity is just a fancy way of saying how much water is in the air. Different plants evolved in different environments, meaning some are used to sucking moisture straight from the air (hello, ferns), while others are tough, desert-adapted badasses who think humidity is for the weak (looking at you, cacti).

Here's how it breaks down:

- **Low humidity (20–40%)** – Great for succulents and cacti. If you have humidity-loving plants in these conditions, they're basically suffocating.

- **Moderate humidity (40–60%)** – The happy middle ground for most plants like pothos, rubber plants and monstera.

- **High humidity (60–80%)** – Where tropical divas like calatheas, ferns and anthuriums will thrive.

If you don't match your plant's needs, expect crispy tips, wilting, slow growth and leaves dropping faster than your enthusiasm for misting (more on that below).

THE MISTING DELUSION – THE GREAT HUMIDITY LIE

Let's address the elephant in the room: misting does not fix humidity. It's the plant care equivalent of licking your lips when they're chapped – temporary relief that actually makes things worse.

Here's the truth: misting increases humidity for about 30 seconds to 5 minutes, tops. After that, the moisture evaporates, leaving your plant in exactly the same situation as before. It does nothing to permanently raise humidity in a room.

Worse? If you mist too much, you're creating a perfect breeding ground for fungus and rot – because nothing screams 'healthy plant' like damp leaves rotting in slow motion.

So, if you love misting because it makes you feel like a botanical deity blessing your leafy subjects, carry on – just don't kid yourself that it's actually doing anything long-term.

REAL HUMIDITY SOLUTIONS – WHAT ACTUALLY WORKS

Since misting is about as useful as a chocolate teapot, what does work? Here are the real game-changers:

HUMIDIFIERS – THE POWER MOVE

If you're serious about humidity, this is the best solution. A humidifier actually adds moisture to the air and maintains stable levels, making it the ultimate fix for fussy tropical plants.

Best For: Calatheas, anthuriums, ferns, alocasias – anything that throws a tantrum the second the air dries out.

Pro Tip: Use filtered or distilled water in your humidifier to prevent mineral buildup on your plants' leaves. If you see a white dust forming? That's hard water residue, and it's not doing your plants any favours.

PEBBLE TRAYS – THE BUDGET HACK

This old-school method involves placing a tray of water and pebbles under your plant. As the water evaporates, it slightly increases local humidity. Emphasis on slightly.

Best For: Plants that appreciate humidity but don't need it cranked up to 100.

Pro Tip: Your plant's pot shouldn't sit in the water – otherwise, congratulations, you've just created a perfect root rot factory.

PROPAGATION BOXES AND MINI GREENHOUSES – THE CONTROL FREAK'S PARADISE

If you're all about high humidity with minimal effort, propagation boxes and enclosed terrariums are your best friends. They trap moisture inside a sealed environment, creating a stable, self-sustaining humidity bubble.

Best For: Baby plants, cuttings, orchids, ferns and anything that thrives in tropical conditions.

Pro Tip: Vent them occasionally to avoid mould or mildew, which love stagnant, damp air.

GROUPING PLANTS TOGETHER – STRENGTH IN NUMBERS

Plants naturally release moisture into the air, so clustering them together creates a microclimate with slightly higher humidity. Think of it like a plant support group – together they're stronger (and less crispy).

Best For: Medium-humidity plants like pothos, philodendrons and rubber plants.

AIR QUALITY – THE SECRET WEAPON FOR HEALTHY PLANTS

Now, let's talk airflow – because humidity without good ventilation is like a gym with no windows. Gross.

VENTILATION: KEEP THE AIR MOVING

- Stagnant air is a breeding ground for mould, pests and diseases. Good airflow keeps things fresh and discourages nasties from settling in.

- If possible, open windows or use a small fan to circulate air around your plants. (Your plants want a gentle breeze, not hurricane-level winds.)

CLEANING YOUR PLANTS – YES, THEY GET DUSTY TOO

- Dust blocks sunlight and hinders photosynthesis (see page 172). Give your plants a gentle wipe-down with a damp cloth to keep their leaves clean.

- For delicate foliage, a soft brush or a light shower can do the trick.

AVOIDING MOULD AND FUNGAL ISSUES

- Overcrowding plants + high humidity + no airflow = disaster.

- Make sure there's space between plants and monitor for mould in high-humidity areas.

THE PERSONALITY TEST: WHICH HUMIDITY HACK IS RIGHT FOR YOU?

THE TECH ENTHUSIAST

You love gadgets, and your humidifier has a remote control? You need calatheas, anthuriums and ferns – the drama queens of the plant world that demand you maintain their perfect environment.

THE NATURALIST

You prefer low-maintenance methods like grouping plants together and letting nature do its thing? Philodendrons, peace lilies and spider plants will fit right into your relaxed, jungle-style approach.

THE LAID-BACK PLANT PARENT

You want zero effort? Pothos, snake plants and rubber plants are your go-to. They don't demand constant humidity and thrive even if you occasionally forget about them.

THE MICROCLIMATE CREATOR

You love mini greenhouses, prop boxes and controlled setups? Your plants of choice are hoyas, orchids, begonias and rare aroids – all of which love enclosed, humid environments.

FINAL THOUGHTS: CREATING THE PERFECT ATMOSPHERE

Humidity and air quality make or break your indoor jungle. If you get it right, your plants will reward you with lush, healthy growth. If you get it wrong? Say hello to crispy, wilting, sad leaves.

Ditch misting, embrace real humidity solutions and pay attention to airflow. Your plants aren't just decorations – they're living things with specific needs. Treat them right and they'll thrive. Ignore them, and they'll show you exactly what disappointment looks like in plant form.

So go forth, tweak your setup and get your indoor atmosphere as close to a tropical paradise as possible – without having to live in a greenhouse yourself.

Spathiphyllum 'Aurea'

Dealing with Plant Stress

Plants don't scream when they're stressed. They don't sigh, roll their eyes or dramatically throw themselves on the floor in protest. But trust me, if they could, some of them absolutely would. Instead, they give us subtle (and sometimes not-so-subtle) signs that something isn't right – leaves turning yellow, tips crisping up like overcooked chips, entire branches deciding they've had enough and dropping off overnight.

The good news? Plants are incredibly resilient. They might throw a tantrum, but they also want to survive, and if you learn to read their signals, you can step in before things go full-blown plant emergency.

The bad news? If you ignore the warning signs for too long, things can escalate quickly. What starts as a drooping leaf today could be a root-rotting disaster next week. But don't worry – you're about to learn how to decode your plants' stress signals, fix the issues before they spiral and create a care routine that keeps your leafy companions thriving instead of just surviving.

RECOGNISING THE SIGNS OF PLANT STRESS

A happy plant pushes out new growth, looks lush and generally vibes with its environment. A stressed plant? That's when things start to look off – leaves droop, colours fade and it stops growing like it should. If your plant could scream, this would be the moment it starts yelling in Morse code.

YELLOWING LEAVES

This is the plant world's equivalent of a warning light on your car dashboard. If the lower leaves are turning yellow, overwatering is usually the culprit – roots drowning in excess moisture, suffocating before they can do their job. But if the yellowing is happening on new growth, your plant might be starving, lacking essential nutrients to sustain healthy development. A general pale or washed-out look? That's your plant begging for more light.

BROWN, CRISPY LEAF EDGES

Classic sign of low humidity. Your plant is drying out faster than a bad fake tan. But don't be fooled – crispy edges can also come from underwatering, exposure to draughts, or even salt buildup from fertilisers. If your calatheas are looking fried, chances are they're throwing a humidity tantrum.

DROOPING LEAVES

This is one of the trickiest stress signals to decode because it could mean one of two completely opposite things: thirst or drowning. If the soil is bone dry, your plant needs a drink, stat. But if it's still damp and the plant looks just as sad, you might have been a little too generous with the watering can.

STUNTED GROWTH

This is like a plant hitting the pause button. If it's barely growing, chances are it's missing something essential – light, nutrients or breathable soil. Compacted, dense soil can also suffocate roots, making it hard for them to take up water and nutrients.

LEAF DROP

The ultimate diva move. Some plants, like the infamous fiddle-leaf fig, will shed leaves just because you looked at them the wrong way. But for most plants, sudden leaf drop signals a problem – temperature swings, relocation shock, inconsistent watering or even pests taking up residence.

WILTING

This is another big red flag, usually linked to dehydration or extreme heat. If your plant is wilting despite moist soil, root damage or poor airflow could be the issue. When roots aren't healthy, no amount of watering will fix it.

PESTS

And then there's the sneaky enemy – pests. If you notice strange discoloured spots, tiny holes, webbing or a weird sticky residue on your plant, you're dealing with an infestation. Spider mites, mealybugs, thrips – they feed by sucking the life out of your plant, leaving behind visible battle scars. Always check under the leaves, in the nooks of stems and even in the soil. If you catch them early, you can fight back before they do serious damage (see page 67).

Bottom line? Your plants are always trying to communicate with you. You just need to learn how to listen.

COMMON CAUSES OF PLANT STRESS AND SOLUTIONS

ENVIRONMENTAL SHIFTS

What It Is: Moving a plant to a new location, changing its pot or sudden shifts in light, temperature or humidity can shock the plant.

How to Fix It: Minimise sudden environmental changes. When repotting or relocating, give the plant time to adapt. Gradual changes, such as slowly introducing a plant to new light levels, can help it settle in more comfortably.

OVERWATERING AND UNDERWATERING

What It Is: Overwatering or underwatering disrupts the balance plants need and can stress roots.

How to Fix It: Tailor watering frequency to each plant and use the 'weight test' to guide you. If a pot feels light and the soil is dry, it's time to water. Use pots with drainage holes to prevent water pooling.

PESTS

What It Is: Pests like spider mites, aphids and mealybugs can drain a plant's energy, leading to signs of stress like discoloured leaves, wilting or sticky residue.

How to Fix It: Regularly inspect plants for pests and remove them at the first sign of infestation. Use natural remedies like neem oil (see page 70) or insecticidal soap for mild cases. For ongoing pest control, ensure good air circulation and maintain overall plant health to make them more resistant to pests.

LIGHT IMBALANCE

What It Is: Plants exposed to too much or too little light often display signs of stress, like leaf burn or yellowing.

How to Fix It: Ensure each plant receives adequate light. For low-light conditions, use grow lights to support healthy growth, and for plants in direct sun, provide some filtering, like a sheer curtain, to avoid leaf burn.

NUTRIENT DEFICIENCY

What It Is: Lack of essential nutrients can lead to symptoms such as yellowing leaves and stunted growth.

How to Fix It: Use a balanced fertiliser during the growing season (see page 60). Adjust the type and amount of fertiliser based on the plant's needs; for instance, foliage plants benefit from higher nitrogen, while flowering plants need more phosphorus.

TEMPERATURE SWINGS

What It Is: Extreme or fluctuating temperatures can shock plants, particularly tropical species.

How to Fix It: Keep plants away from sources of extreme temperatures like draughty windows or heaters. A stable temperature range of 18–24°C (65–75°F) is ideal for most indoor plants.

Monstera pinnatipartita

CREATING A RELAXED ENVIRONMENT FOR YOUR PLANTS

Creating a calm, stable environment is essential to keeping stress at bay and ensuring plants flourish. Here are a few ways to maintain conditions that support long-term health:

- **Routine is key** – Establish a consistent care routine for watering, feeding and light exposure. Plants benefit from a stable environment just as much as they do from sunlight and water.
- **Humidity control** – For tropical plants, consider a humidifier or using pebble trays to maintain the right humidity levels, especially in dry winter months (see page 86).
- **Good airflow** – Air circulation is crucial for preventing pests and mould (see page 88). Open windows when possible or use a small fan to keep the air moving gently around your plants.
- **Practise patience and adapt** – Plants, like people, need time to adjust to changes. Avoid moving plants around too often or exposing them to sudden environmental shifts, as this can lead to shock.

KEEP IT MANAGEABLE: A HOBBY, NOT A HASSLE

Plant care should bring joy and fulfilment, not stress. As with any passion, maintaining a healthy balance is key. If caring for plants feels overwhelming or if you're taking on too much, it's okay to scale back. Start small and gradually add plants as you build confidence and develop your care routine. This approach will help keep plant care manageable, allowing you to truly enjoy the journey of nurturing each plant.

Remember, plants have their own rhythm, and so should you. Celebrate the small wins, like new leaves and healthy growth, and let go of any setbacks. You'll be rewarded with a flourishing indoor jungle and a lifelong love for this green world.

THE PERSONALITY TEST: HOW YOU HANDLE PLANT STRESS

We all have different styles when it comes to plant care. Where do you fit?

THE CALMING MINIMALIST

You like low-maintenance plants that thrive on neglect. Snake plants, ZZ plants and pothos are your best friends because they forgive your occasional forgetfulness.

THE TROPICAL CAREGIVER

You're obsessed with lush, jungle vibes and aren't afraid of high-maintenance plants. Ferns, calatheas and alocasias challenge you, but that's part of the fun.

THE OBSERVATION ENTHUSIAST

You love watching plants closely, spotting small changes and tweaking conditions to keep them thriving. Fiddle-leaf figs, monsteras and philodendrons are perfect for you because they reward attention with dramatic growth.

THE GO-WITH-THE-FLOW PARENT

You're chill, flexible and don't stress over imperfections. You'll do well with adaptable plants like spider plants, rubber plants and dracaenas that can handle a bit of inconsistency.

Philodendron burle marxii 'Variegata'

FINAL THOUGHTS:
LEARN, ADAPT AND KEEP GROWING

Plant care isn't about getting it perfect – it's about learning and adapting. Every stressed plant teaches you something. Maybe you overwatered because you didn't check the soil. Maybe you placed a light-loving plant in a dim corner. Maybe you moved your fiddle-leaf fig and now it's dropping leaves like it's throwing a tantrum. Whatever it is, you'll figure it out, adjust and do better next time.

And that's the beauty of plant care. It's not about having a perfect jungle where nothing ever goes wrong – it's about learning from the journey, growing alongside your plants and knowing that even when things go sideways, there's almost always a way back.

So, if a plant is looking rough, don't panic. Check the signs, make the adjustments and keep going. That's what this whole thing is about – progress, not perfection.

Every stressed plant teaches you something

SEASONAL PLANT CARE: DOES IT EVEN MATTER?

Let's be honest – most people think of seasonal plant care like flipping a switch: Spring? More water. Summer? Even more water. Winter? Stop touching your plants. But here's the thing – your plants aren't staring at a calendar thinking, Ah yes, March 21st. Time to grow. They react to light, temperature and humidity, not human-made seasons.

If your house is a tropical paradise of grow lights, humidifiers and controlled temperatures, your plants couldn't care less whether it's snowing outside. They're living in a year-round, artificially created utopia where seasons don't exist. But if your plants rely on natural light and your house mimics the Arctic in winter, then yeah, seasons matter.

So, let's break this down the right way – by the conditions that actually change rather than pretending your plants care about months on a calendar.

LIGHT: THE ULTIMATE SEASONAL FACTOR

Light is the biggest game-changer when it comes to seasonal shifts. Winter means shorter, weaker daylight hours, and summer brings long, bright exposure. If your plants depend on natural light, they'll react to these changes, slowing down in winter and exploding in growth during summer.

What You Can Do:

- **Winter** – Move plants closer to windows, clean your windows (seriously, dirt blocks light) and consider grow lights if it gets ridiculously dark.

- **Summer** – Watch out for scorching sun. If your south-facing window turns into a death ray, use sheer curtains or move plants slightly away.

- **Grow light crew** – You don't need to change anything – your plants are in an endless summer. Just keep an eye on light duration – 14–16 hours are usually plenty.

TEMPERATURE: NOT TOO HOT, NOT TOO COLD

Unless you're living in a greenhouse, your home's temperature changes between seasons. Heaters crank up in winter, windows get thrown open in summer and your plants feel every bit of it.

What You Can Do:

- **Winter** – Keep plants away from radiators, fireplaces and draughts. Nothing says instant death like a plant chilling near a frosty window or roasting on a radiator.

- **Summer** – If you're blasting AC, it can dry out the air. If your house turns into a sauna, your plants will either love it (tropicals rejoice) or hate it (cacti scream internally).

- **Controlled environments** – If you're regulating temps with heaters and humidifiers, you've already cracked the code. Just watch out for sudden fluctuations – plants hate those (see page 95).

Epipremnum pinnatum albo variegata

WATERING: STOP DROWNING OR STARVING THEM

Here's where people screw up the most. Seasonal watering isn't about following a strict schedule – it's about observing how your plant is behaving.

The Golden Rule: If the soil is still wet, don't water it. If it's dry, water it. Revolutionary, I know.

What You Can Do:

- **Winter** – Most plants need way less water because they grow slower. Overwatering in winter is the leading cause of plant deaths (RIP root rot victims).

- **Summer** – Water more frequently if the soil dries out faster. But don't assume all plants need more – some prefer to dry out between waterings.

- **Humidity-controlled setup** – If your humidity and temps are stable, your watering routine can stay consistent year-round.

Snake plant

HUMIDITY: THE SILENT KILLER (OR HEALER)

Humidity levels plummet in winter when heaters suck every last drop of moisture from the air. If your plants have crispy edges and look like they've been through a dehydration challenge, this is why. Conversely, in summer, humidity can spike, making some plants thrive while others (looking at you, succulents) start sulking.

What You Can Do:

- **Winter** – If your house is drier than the Sahara, get a humidifier. Pebble trays and misting won't cut it (I've ranted about this before).

- **Summer** – If humidity climbs, ensure airflow is good to prevent mould, fungus and pests.

- **If you've created a controlled jungle** – Humidity doesn't change – good job, you've hacked the system.

GROWTH AND FERTILISING: TO FEED OR NOT TO FEED?

Plants slow down in winter and speed up in spring/summer – unless you've created an artificial Eden where they grow year-round. Feeding plants that aren't actively growing is like force-feeding someone while they're asleep – not helpful, and probably harmful.

What You Can Do:

- **Winter** – Skip the fertiliser unless your plant is actively pushing out new growth.

- **Spring/summer** – If your plant is shooting out leaves like it's had an espresso, give it a nutrient boost.

- **Artificial setups** – If your plants are growing year-round, feed lightly and consistently. No need for seasonal shifts.

To feed or not to feed

THE PERSONALITY TEST:
WHAT KIND OF YEAR-ROUND PLANT PARENT ARE YOU?

THE SEASONAL SYMPATHISER

You follow the rhythms of nature, adjusting care through the seasons. Your plants experience winter dormancy, spring awakenings and summer explosions. You probably own alocasias, anthuriums and ferns that actually need the shifts.

THE YEAR-ROUND GROWER

You've created an indoor jungle that ignores seasons. Your plants never rest thanks to grow lights, humidifiers and stable temps. You're probably a philodendron, monstera and pothos hoarder who enjoys endless green.

THE SET-AND-FORGET MINIMALIST

You don't adjust anything. Your ZZ plant, snake plant and cast-iron plant thrive on neglect, no matter the season. Your plant care style is *vibes only*.

Monstera deliciosa

FINAL THOUGHTS: DO WHAT WORKS FOR YOU

At the end of the day, your home's environment dictates everything. If you're running a controlled setup, seasonal shifts barely matter. If you rely on natural conditions, your care should adjust accordingly.

The real key? Observe your plants. They'll tell you what they need – crispy leaves, yellowing or slowed growth aren't seasonal flukes, they're clues. Learn their language and you'll never be scrambling to 'winter-proof' your plants again.

No strict rules, no stress – just plants, thriving in the world you create for them.

No strict rules, no stress – just plants, thriving in the world you create for them

LEVEL 5
PLANT WHISPERER

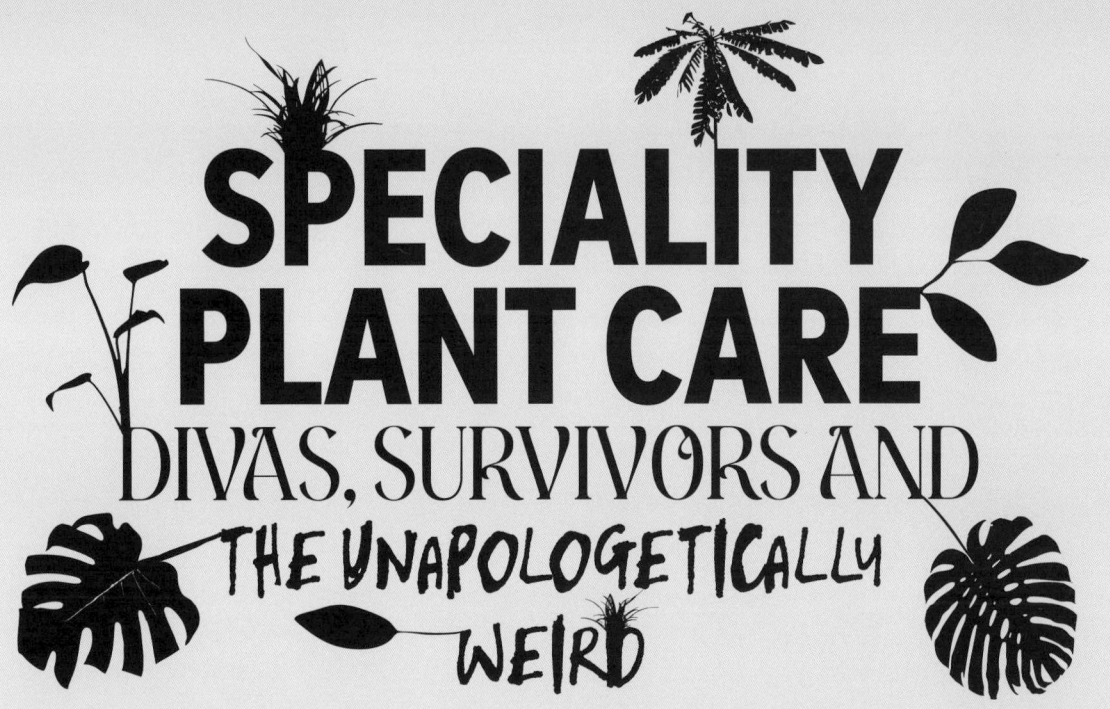

SPECIALITY PLANT CARE
DIVAS, SURVIVORS AND THE UNAPOLOGETICALLY WEIRD

Not all plants are created equal. Some are as easy-going as a ZZ plant left in a dark corner, while others demand rainforest-level conditions and scream diva energy at the slightest inconvenience. Some can go weeks without a drop of water, and others would rather die dramatically than miss a single misting.

This chapter is your VIP access pass into the world of specialty plants – the high-maintenance queens, the desert-dwelling badasses, the creatures of pure humidity and the straight-up bizarre. Whether you're looking to expand your collection or just want to know which plants will test your patience the most, we're diving in.

THE SUPREME HUMIDITY LOVERS: THE GLASSHOUSE GODS

If humidity was a currency, these plants would be billionaires. They don't just like humidity, they require it to survive. If you can't provide 80–90% humidity, these might not be for you (unless you love watching leaves crisp up and die in real-time).

Who They Are:

- **Terrarium plants** – Mini humidity fiends like fittonias, mosses, jewel orchids and ferns.
- **High-humidity orchids** – Dracula orchids, masdevallias and some bulbophyllums – these aren't your standard phalaenopsis.
- **Select anthuriums** – *A. warocqueanum* and *A. veitchii*, aka the ones that look like they belong in a fantasy film.

What They Need:

- **Humidity never dropping below 80%** – They can be acclimatised by gradually reducing their humidity over a few weeks.
- **Terrariums, prop boxes or sealed environments** – Where moisture is locked in.
- **No dry air** – These plants have zero tolerance for dry air. Even a central heating vent nearby can ruin their day.

Personality match?
You're a perfectionist who enjoys the challenge of getting conditions just right. You don't just care for plants – you create microclimates.

TAMING THE GODS

Acclimatising a high-humidity-loving plant to the average UK home (which typically hovers around 50–60% humidity) is all about gradual adaptation and reducing stress. If you throw a humidity addict like an anthurium, jewel orchid or delicate fern straight into your living room without a transition plan, expect some dramatic tantrums – crispy edges, drooping leaves or straight-up plant rebellion. The best approach is to slowly wean it off extreme humidity levels over a few weeks. Start by keeping it in a controlled high-humidity environment (like a prop box, greenhouse cabinet or plastic dome) and gradually introduce more airflow by venting it for longer periods each day. If you're moving it from a propagation box, start with just an hour or two outside before returning it to safety. Increase this exposure daily until it's living full-time in regular home humidity. Group it with other plants, use a pebble tray or place it near a humidifier to soften the transition. Most importantly, watch for signs of stress – if it's losing too much moisture too quickly, slow the process down. Some plants will adapt fully, others might always need a little extra humidity love, but a careful introduction means fewer crispy leaf funerals along the way.

Anthurium bonplandii 'Variegata'

Rhaphidophora tetrasperma

THE JUNGLE TIER: PHILODENDRONS, MONSTERAS, RHAPHIDOPHORAS AND SYNGONIUMS

These plants still love humidity but aren't quite as insane about it as the glasshouse gods above. From 60–80% humidity is ideal, and they'll tolerate slightly lower levels if you give them good care.

Who They Are:

- **Philodendrons** – Including *P. gloriosum*, *P. melanochrysum* and the classic heartleaf philodendron.
- **Monsteras** – *M. deliciosa*, *M. adansonii* and their fancy variegated cousins.
- **Rhaphidophoras and syngoniums** – The fast-growing, vining jungle creepers that climb anything they touch.

What They Need:

- **Moderate to high humidity** – Keep it at 60%+ for best results.
- **Good airflow** – Stagnant air encourages rot and fungal issues.
- **Climbing support** – These plants want to grow upwards. Give them a moss pole or they'll try climbing your furniture.

Personality match?
You love fast growers, statement foliage and plants that reward you with dramatic, lush growth if you get the conditions right.

THE CASUAL HUMIDITY APPRECIATORS: AROIDS, PEACE LILIES AND SOME FERNS

These plants like humidity but won't throw a tantrum if you don't mist them daily. They do best in the 40–60% humidity range, which is achievable in most homes without any special setups.

Who They Are:

- **Common anthuriums** – Not the rare collectors' pieces, but solid, dependable anthuriums like *Anthurium andraeanum*.
- **Peace lilies** – Gorgeous when happy, the ultimate passive-aggressive sulkers when not.
- **Boston ferns and maidenhair ferns** – A little fussy, but not impossible.

What They Need:

- **Even moisture** – They hate drying out completely.
- **Humidity around 50%+** – They'll tolerate less but expect brown tips.
- **Some patience** – Especially with peace lilies, which will pretend to die if you forget them for more than a week.

Personality match?
You want something a little more involved than a snake plant but don't have time to babysit the true divas.

Syngonium podophyllum 'Mojito'

THE DRY LOVERS: SUCCULENTS, CACTI AND DESERT CHAMPIONS

These plants hate humidity. They thrive in dry, airy environments and need fast-draining soil to prevent root rot.

Who They Are:

- **Cacti** – The kings of survival, found thriving in the harshest deserts on earth.
- **Echeveria and haworthia** – Rosette-forming succulents that hate being overwatered.
- **Jade plants and aloe vera** – Chunky, water-storing legends that thrive on neglect.

What They Need:

- **Bright, direct sunlight** – Low light is a death sentence.
- **Sandy, gritty soil** – Water retention is the enemy of these plants.
- **No humidity traps** – Keep them out of closed terrariums unless you want to watch them rot.

Personality match?
You appreciate independence and don't want to be tied to a strict watering schedule. You respect plants that thrive on resilience.

THE FREAKS OF NATURE: CARNIVOROUS PLANTS AND AIR PLANTS

CARNIVOROUS PLANTS – THE MURDERERS

These plants hunt. They evolved in nutrient-poor soil, so they adapted by eating bugs.

Who They Are:

- **Venus flytraps** – Dramatic as hell but rewarding.
- **Pitcher plants** – Nature's fly traps – elegant, deadly and perfect for keeping pests in check.
- **Sundews** – Sticky and effective at trapping unsuspecting insects.

What They Need:

- **Distilled water or rainwater** – Tap water kills them.
- **Full sun** – Without it, they will just sit there, sulking.
- **Wet soil** – They live in bogs, so they don't mind being constantly damp.

Personality match? You like weird, unusual plants that offer entertainment and practicality.

AIR PLANTS – THE SOIL HATERS

Air plants don't need soil. They absorb water through their leaves, living off the moisture in the air.

Who They Are:

- **Tillandsia:** The epiphytes that cling to surfaces like rebels of the plant world.

What They Need:

- **Bright, indirect light** – Too much shade = slow death.
- **Regular misting or soaking** – Because they drink through their leaves.
- **Good airflow** – Otherwise, rot city.

Personality match? You enjoy unconventional plants and want something different from the usual potted setup.

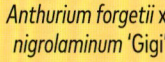

Anthurium forgetii x nigrolaminum 'Gigi'

FINAL THOUGHTS: CHOOSE YOUR SPECIALITY PLANTS WISELY

Whether you're into lush, high-maintenance tropicals, easy-going succulents or carnivorous freaks, every specialty plant comes with its quirks. Know what you're getting into before you commit and remember – at the end of the day, plant care should be fun, not stressful.

If it's making you miserable, ditch the diva and find something that fits your lifestyle.

Because, let's be real – not every plant deserves a place in your kingdom.

Not every plant deserves a place in your kingdom

PRUNING
AND TRAINING AND GOING FULL JUNGLE MODE

Imagine if you never got a haircut. Ever. Just let everything grow wild, unchecked – split ends everywhere, hair sticking out at weird angles, slowly turning into a human tumbleweed. Some people (like myself) might vibe with that look. Others? Not so much.

Plants are the same. Some thrive in their chaos, looking better when they sprawl unchecked, while others need a bit of shaping to bring out their best form. But pruning and training aren't just about keeping your plants looking good – they can completely change the way they grow, how fast they mature and even the shape, colour and size of their leaves. In some cases, training a plant to climb can trigger an evolution that'll blow your mind – turning dinky, juvenile leaves into massive, fenestrated beasts that look like they belong in a prehistoric rainforest.

And if you're ready to go full jungle, why stop at moss poles? Your house itself can become the support system – walls, beams, pipes and furniture transformed into climbing frames for a living, breathing green masterpiece.

But first, let's talk about why we prune and train in the first place.

THE POWER OF PRUNING: WHY IT'S ESSENTIAL

Pruning isn't just about aesthetics. It's a tactical move – cutting in the right places makes your plants stronger, encourages lush new growth, prevents disease and redirects energy to where it's needed most. Pruning is like giving your plants a motivational speech.

Here's what pruning does:

- **Encourages new growth** – Removing dead or weak parts tells the plant to push out fresh, healthy leaves and branches.
- **Prevents disease and pests** – Sickly or damaged leaves attract trouble. Cut them off before they cause problems.
- **Shapes your plant** – If your monstera is growing like a drunk octopus, pruning helps guide it into something more controlled.
- **Stops leggy growth** – When plants stretch for light and get spindly, strategic cuts can make them bushier.
- **Redirects energy** – Plants can waste energy on unnecessary growth. A good prune tells them where to focus.

TOOLS OF THE TRADE: DON'T HACK AWAY WITH KITCHEN SCISSORS

Using blunt or dirty tools is the fastest way to mess up your plant and invite infections. Invest in sharp, clean equipment:

- **Pruning shears** – For thick stems and branches, especially on bigger plants like rubber trees.
- **Fine-tipped scissors** – For delicate work, like trimming soft leaves or flowers.
- **Bypass loppers** – For heavy-duty cuts on larger, woody stems.
- **Sterilising wipes/alcohol** – Always clean your tools before and after pruning to avoid spreading bacteria or pests.

Pro Tip: If you hear crunching when you cut, your tool is too dull. Get those blades sharpened.

PRUNING TECHNIQUES: HOW TO CUT LIKE A PRO

- **Deadheading** – Snip off dead flowers and leaves to keep energy focused on new growth. **Great For:** Peace lilies, African violets and orchids.
- **Pinching** – Remove the very tip of a stem with your fingers or scissors to make the plant bushier. **Perfect For:** Pothos, basil and coleus.
- **Cutting back (hard pruning)** – Chop off a large section of growth to encourage fresh, vigorous regrowth. **Best For:** Leggy monstera, rubber plants and jade trees.
- **Selective pruning** – Remove specific branches to shape your plant and control its size. **Great For:** Bonsai, ficus or philodendrons.
- **Thinning** – Remove excess foliage to improve airflow and reduce the risk of disease. **Essential For:** Dense plants like ferns and monsteras.

TRAINING: WHEN PLANTS LEVEL UP AND BECOME BEASTS

Pruning helps plants grow, but training completely changes how they grow. Some plants naturally sprawl, while others are climbers that need a structure to reach their full potential. The way you train them can turn a small plant into a towering jungle feature.

Here's how:

- **Staking and supporting** – Use stakes, moss poles or trellises to guide plants upwards. **Great For:** Monstera, philodendrons and hoyas.
- **Climbing and trailing** – Guide vines along walls, shelves or hanging hooks. **Try It With:** Pothos, string of hearts or ivy.
- **Espalier** – Training plants to grow flat against a surface, like a trellis or wall.
- **Twisting and wiring** – Bonsai lovers, this one's for you. Gently bend stems or use soft wire to shape a plant's growth. **Used In:** bonsai and artistic plant shaping.

And Here's the Real Magic: Some plants unlock their final form when they climb.

Monstera, philodendron and epipremnum all start life with small, juvenile leaves. But when you give them something to climb, their leaves transform – bigger, bolder and sometimes completely different in shape and colour. A monstera that's crawling along the ground might only grow small, solid leaves, but train it up a moss pole, and suddenly you're getting those iconic, fenestrated jungle leaves.

Climbing isn't just aesthetic – it's evolutionary. In the wild, these plants grow towards the light by climbing trees. When they reach a certain height, their leaves mature and become far more dramatic. If you want your plants to hit beast mode, give them something to climb

COOL PLANT FACT:

Those iconic holes and splits – called fenestrations – in mature plants like the monstera aren't just for show. They're nature's way of letting light filter down to the lower leaves, like a living skylight system. It's the plant looking after itself, making sure every part still gets a piece of the sun. Self-care, jungle style.

GOING FULL JUNGLE: USING YOUR HOME AS A SUPPORT SYSTEM

Why settle for just moss poles and trellises when you can use your entire house as a climbing frame? This is how you take plant styling from 'nice houseplants' to living rainforest.

- **Walls and ceilings** – Use removable hooks or wall mounts to guide climbing plants along walls.
- **Beams and pipes** – Let trailing plants cascade down exposed beams or wrap around pipes.
- **Bookshelves and furniture** – Train vines to weave through shelving or drape dramatically over furniture.
- **DIY living walls** – Attach grid panels or wooden slats to walls for plants to climb.

This isn't just about making your home look like a jungle – it's about letting plants grow the way they're meant to. The more closely you can mimic their natural environment, the more they'll thrive.

THE PERSONALITY TEST: WHAT'S YOUR PRUNING AND TRAINING STYLE?

THE JUNGLE ARCHITECT

You want a full rainforest in your living room. Your monstera has three moss poles, and your walls are covered in trailing plants.

THE MINIMALIST SCULPTOR

Clean lines, sleek shapes. Your fiddle-leaf fig is pruned into a perfect silhouette.

THE ARTISTIC GROWER

You train bonsai, shape ivy into spirals and dream of espalier fruit trees.

THE CHAOS LOVER

Your plants do what they want. You prune when you remember, and training is optional.

Rhaphidophora tetrasperma

FINAL THOUGHTS: CUT, SHAPE AND WATCH THE MAGIC HAPPEN

Pruning and training aren't just maintenance – they're tools for shaping your plant kingdom. Whether you want a structured, architectural look or a wild jungle sprawling across your ceiling, learning to cut with confidence and train with intention will take your plant game to another level.

So, grab your shears, get to work and remember – sometimes, the wildest transformations happen with just one snip.

Pruning is like giving your plants a motivational speech

REPOTTING AND ROOT CARE DIGGING: DEEP INTO PLANT SURVIVAL

Roots: underground warriors of plant life. Silent architects of survival. The part of a plant you rarely see, yet the most important part of all.

Without strong, healthy roots, your plants are basically doomed. You can give them all the fancy pots, filtered water and lovingly whispered affirmations you want – if the roots aren't thriving, the rest of the plant won't either.

And yet, how often do we actually check on them? Most people repot only when their plant starts looking miserable, not realising that by the time a plant's foliage is screaming for help, the roots have probably been suffering in silence for months. It's time to change that.

This chapter is all about getting under the soil – literally. We're diving into the when, why and how of repotting, how to keep roots in top form, how to prevent the dreaded hydrophobic soil, and what to do when your plant's root system turns into an apocalyptic mess.

And, before we even get into it, if you haven't yet read Chapter 5 – the soil mix chapter (see page 47) – go check it out. The right soil mix can mean the difference between a plant that thrives and one that throws in the towel after a month. Whether you're dealing with a tropical jungle beast, a desert dweller or something in between, getting the mix right from the start will save you a world of trouble later.

WHY REPOTTING MATTERS – IT'S NOT JUST ABOUT SIZE

A lot of people think repotting is just about getting a bigger pot. Wrong. Repotting is a full-on reset. It's like giving your plant a fresh lease on life – a new bed, fresh food and a chance to shake off whatever's been holding it back.

Here's what makes repotting essential:

- **Soil goes stale** – Over time, soil loses structure, compresses and turns into a suffocating, lifeless mass. It's like trying to breathe in a vacuum. Fresh soil means fresh nutrients, aeration and better drainage.

- **Roots need room** – When roots start circling the pot like they're stuck in a traffic jam, they stop functioning properly. Without space to stretch, they can't absorb nutrients efficiently, leading to stunted growth.

- **Disease and pests lurk below** – Root rot, fungus gnats, hidden pests – you name it. If you never check, you'll never know what's brewing beneath the surface.

- **Hydrophobic soil can sneak up on you** – Ever watered a plant only to see the water rush straight through without actually soaking in? That's what happens when soil gets too dry or too compacted.

SIGNS YOUR PLANT IS BEGGING FOR A REPOT

Plants don't have mouths, but they sure as hell know how to communicate. Here are the telltale signs that your plant is desperate for a bigger home:

- **Roots coming out of the drainage holes** – If roots are trying to escape, they're literally out of room.

- **Soil drying out way too fast** – If you water your plant and it dries out within a day, chances are the roots have taken over the pot.

- **Water running straight through** – A classic sign of hydrophobic soil or root compaction.

- **Stunted growth, yellowing or wilting** – If your plant has stopped growing in peak season, the roots may be strangling themselves.

And the Biggest Sign? If you pull the plant out of its pot and see a solid mass of tangled roots with barely any soil left, that's what we call root-bound hell.

THE ART OF REPOTTING: HOW TO GIVE YOUR PLANT A FRESH START

If you've ever had to move house, you know it's a mission. Moving plants is no different. Here's how to do it right:

1. Choose the right pot – Bigger isn't always better. A new pot should be 5–10 cm (2–4 inches) wider than the old one – too big and the extra soil will stay soggy, leading to rot.

2. Gently remove the plant – Turn the pot sideways, squeeze the sides (if it's plastic) or tap the bottom to ease the plant out. If it refuses to budge, run a knife along the inside edge.

3. Check and loosen the roots – If the roots are circling like they're stuck in an endless queue, tease them apart gently. For severely root-bound plants, you may need to cut a few to encourage outward growth.

4. Refresh the soil – Use a mix tailored to your plant. If you're not sure what that is, flip back to pages 50–53 for a breakdown of the best blends for different plants. Aroids? Everyday mix. Succulents? Gritty and fast draining. Orchids? Bark-heavy.

5. Position and fill – Sit the plant at the same depth as before, then fill in around it with fresh soil. Tap the pot gently to settle everything in place.

6. Water thoroughly – This helps the soil settle and gets rid of air pockets. Make sure it drains properly.

FUNNY THOUGHT:

In nature, plants don't have pots. No terracotta prisons. No trendy ceramics. So the idea that some plants need to be root-bound? Yeah … I'm not buying it. Personally, I pot straight into a bigger home. Why? Because I've got a life to live and I don't want to repot the same plant every year like it's Groundhog Day with soil. But here's the catch: a bigger pot means more soil. More soil holds more water. If your plant has baby roots and you're heavy-handed with watering, you might create the perfect storm for root rot. Think soggy death trap with drainage holes. So unless you really know your plants, stick to a small step up in size. It's safer, less drama and your plant won't send you hate mail in the form of yellow leaves.

THE ROOT DIAGNOSIS TEST

What's going on below the soil? Take this quick test to diagnose your plant's root situation and discover its Root Personality – along with the best repotting strategy!

WHEN YOU LIFT YOUR PLANT OUT OF THE POT, WHAT DO THE ROOTS LOOK LIKE?

- Tightly circling the pot → You've got a root-bound plant! Time to upsize and loosen those roots.
- Black, mushy, and smelly → Root rot detected! Trim the damage, let it dry out before repotting.
- Sparse, barely filling the pot → Might be over-potted! Keep it in the same size pot with fresh soil or even size down.
- Thick and healthy but growing through drainage holes → Perfectly happy but needs more legroom. Upgrade to a slightly bigger pot!

WHEN YOU WATER, HOW QUICKLY DOES IT DRAIN?

- Water sits on top and drains slowly → Your mix is too dense! Add aeration (perlite, bark, or pumice).
- It flows right through immediately → Too loose! Consider adding some moisture-retaining elements like worm castings or compost.
- Takes a reasonable time to absorb → Your soil mix is golden. Don't fix what isn't broken!

WHAT'S YOUR PLANT'S ROOT PERSONALITY?

The Wild Wanderer
Fast grower, loves fresh soil and frequent repotting.

- If your plant fills the pot fast, sends out runners, and loves fresh soil, you've got a Wild Wanderer on your hands.
- Best strategy: Repot often, give it space to spread, and don't let it sit in compacted soil.

The Clingy Overachiever
Root-bound and resisting change, but needs a bigger pot.

- If your plant hates repotting but is choking itself in a tiny pot, it's time for an upgrade – even if it protests.
- Best strategy: Loosen the roots gently, upsize one step at a time, and expect a bit of sulking.

The Drama Queen
Sensitive roots that hate being disturbed – handle with care!

- If your plant drops leaves, stops growing, or throws a tantrum every time it's repotted, you've got a Drama Queen.

- Best strategy: Repot only when absolutely necessary, disturb the roots as little as possible, and use a soft, airy mix.

The Lazy Grower
Slow root development, doesn't need frequent repotting.

- If your plant sits in the same pot for years with no complaints, it's a Lazy Grower.

- Best strategy: Keep it in the same pot for as long as possible, only repot when it truly outgrows the space.

FINAL THOUGHTS: THE ROOTS OF SUCCESS

If there's one thing you take from this chapter, let it be this: healthy roots = healthy plants. They're the foundation of everything. If your plant's struggling, start by checking the roots – you'll be amazed at how much they tell you.

And don't forget – soil matters. Before repotting, make sure your mix is spot on (again, see Chapter 5 for best practices). Bad soil can undo all the good work of repotting in one go.

Repot when needed. Keep your soil fresh. Respect the underground network.

And if all else fails? Propagate, start afresh and never stop growing.

Respect the underground network

SUSTAINABLE PLANT CARE: KEEPING YOUR JUNGLE GREEN (FOR REAL)

Plants are supposed to be the eco-friendly hobby, right? You bring a little piece of nature inside, surround yourself with leafy goodness and suddenly, you're a responsible steward of the earth.

Except … maybe not.

Because, let's be honest – modern plant care can be an absolute menace to the environment. Plastic pots stacked up like the aftermath of a garden centre heist. Peat-based soil mixes ripping apart ecosystems one bag at a time. Chemical fertilisers doing God-knows-what to the water supply.

Yeah, we can do better.

The good news? Sustainable plant care isn't just good for the planet – it's better for your plants too. It's about working with nature, not against it. About making choices that keep both your indoor jungle and the wild jungles of the world thriving.

So, let's get into it: how do we make our plant obsession a little less destructive and a whole lot greener?

SOIL THAT DOESN'T SUCK THE LIFE OUT OF THE PLANET

You need soil. Your plants need soil. But what they don't need is peat.

Peat has been the go-to in commercial soil mixes for decades because it holds moisture like a dream. But there's a price: harvesting peat bogs destroys entire ecosystems, releases stored carbon and takes centuries to regenerate. It's like rainforest deforestation, just in a swampier setting.

Thankfully, there are far better alternatives. Coconut coir is one of the best, made from leftover coconut husks that would otherwise be wasted. It holds moisture just as well as peat, but without the environmental destruction. Compost is another hero, whether homemade or store-bought, feeding your soil naturally while reducing waste. Bark and wood chips improve drainage and structure, perfect for tropical plants or orchids, and worm castings add nutrients and beneficial microbes, making your soil truly alive.

Getting the right mix is key. Check out the soil mixes on pages 50–53 for tailored recipes that suit different plant types. Aroids, succulents, ferns – they all need different textures and moisture levels. Nail your soil mix, and you're already halfway to sustainable plant care.

FERTILISING WITHOUT WRECKING THE PLANET

Chemical fertilisers might make your plants pop, but they don't just disappear once you water them in. Excess salts build up in the soil, mess with microbial life and when they inevitably run off, they pollute waterways and disrupt aquatic ecosystems. The better option? Feeding your plants like nature intended.

Banana peels soaked in water create a potassium-rich drink that plants adore. Crushed eggshells provide a slow-release calcium boost. Compost tea – essentially soaking compost in water for a day or two – turns into a powerful, nutrient-rich liquid feed. And if you keep fish, that 'dirty' fish tank water is liquid gold for plants, packed with nitrates that act as a natural fertiliser (see page 77). Just don't use water from a saltwater tank unless you're looking to accidentally murder your entire collection.

What's even better? Using these natural fertilisers keeps the soil alive, unlike synthetic fertilisers, which only provide a quick nutrient hit before fading away. Sustainable plant care means feeding your soil, not just your plants.

Alocasia 'Dragon Scale'

WATERING WITHOUT WASTE

Watering is non-negotiable. But wasting water? Completely avoidable.

One of the simplest tricks is reusing household water. Leftover water from rinsing vegetables? Use it. The stuff you drain from pasta (once it's cooled down)? That too. If you have outdoor space, collecting rainwater is a no-brainer – it's free, natural and far better for plants than tap water.

The way you water also matters. Instead of frequent, shallow watering that barely reaches the roots, water deeply and less often to encourage strong root systems. Overwatering isn't just bad for the environment – it's bad for your plants, leading to root rot, fungus gnats and general misery.

Grouping plants with similar water needs makes life easier too. No more overwatering a cactus while trying to keep your ferns happy. And if you're battling hydrophobic soil – where water just runs off instead of absorbing – check out the repotting and root care information on pages 127–129 for fixes, because that's a problem that needs solving.

ESCAPING THE PLASTIC POT TRAP

Plastic pots. They're cheap, convenient and … absolutely everywhere. The problem? They don't break down. Ever.

The best solution is to ditch plastic where you can or use brands that make recycled plastic pots! Terracotta pots are a solid alternative – breathable, stylish and completely biodegradable. There are also biodegradable pots made from coconut fibre, bamboo or even recycled paper. And if you're feeling creative, old tins, ceramic bowls or even hollowed-out coconuts can all make stunning planters.

If you already have plastic pots, the best thing you can do is reuse them for as long as possible before recycling them properly. The key is to make them last – because the longer they stay in use, the less time they will spend in a landfill.

Watering is non-negotiable

SUSTAINABLE PEST CONTROL (BECAUSE POISONING EVERYTHING IS LAZY)

Pests are inevitable, but nuking them with chemicals isn't the answer. Sustainable pest control is about balance, not overkill.

The easiest fix? Introducing predator mites. These tiny assassins feast on spider mites, thrips and other plant-destroying pests without harming your plants or the environment. Neem oil is another classic – used for centuries as a natural pesticide and fungicide, it keeps things under control without the nasty chemicals. And if you're dealing with something small-scale, a simple DIY soap spray (water + a few drops of washing-up liquid) works wonders (see page 70).

Pest problems are often symptoms, not causes. Overwatering, poor airflow and weak soil health all make plants more vulnerable. Fix those issues, and you'll naturally reduce infestations before they become a nightmare.

PROPAGATION: THE GREENEST HACK IN PLANT CARE

There's nothing more sustainable than growing new plants from what you already have. Instead of constantly buying new plants (which often come in plastic pots and are grown with who-knows-what chemicals), propagation lets you expand your collection for free (see page 75).

Water propagation (see page 161) works beautifully for pothos, philodendrons and monsteras. Prop boxes – high-humidity setups for delicate cuttings – are perfect for trickier plants like anthuriums or alocasias.

Not only does propagation save you money, but it also reduces demand for mass-produced, often unsustainably grown plants. Growing your own means less shipping, less waste and zero guilt.

Reduce infestations before they become a nightmare

THE ECO-GROWER SCORECARD

How sustainable is your plant care? Find out where you stand!

1. What kind of soil do you use?

A) Peat-free mix with organic amendments → Sustainable champion

B) Store-bought mix with peat but trying to change → Sustainability apprentice

C) Whatever is cheapest and easiest → Let's upgrade your game!

3. How do you water your plants?

A) Rainwater or fish tank water → Eco genius!

B) Tap water but let it sit to dechlorinate → Better than nothing!

C) Straight from the tap, no questions asked → There's room for improvement!

2. What do you do with old soil?

A) Reuse and refresh it with compost or worm castings → Zero-waste warrior

B) Toss it but thinking about reusing in the future → Work in progress

C) Bin it without a second thought → Time to rethink – plants thrive in recycled soil!

4. How do you deal with pests?

A) Biological control (predator mites, beneficial insects, neem oil) → Nature's ally!

B) Mild insecticidal soap but open to better methods → Balanced approach

C) Reach for chemicals at the first sign of trouble → Time to explore natural alternatives!

YOUR SUSTAINABILITY RANK

- **Eco Warrior (Mostly As)** – You're a sustainability master! Keep leading by example.
- **Sustainability Apprentice (Mostly Bs)** – You're making solid efforts, but there's still room to grow.
- **Rookie Recycler (Mostly Cs)** – Time to implement small changes – your plants and the planet will thank you!

FINAL THOUGHTS: GROWING GREEN, LIVING GREEN

Let's be clear: sustainable plant care isn't about perfection. You don't have to suddenly start composting banana peels and growing everything in terracotta overnight. But small, conscious choices – ditching peat, using natural fertilisers, watering smarter, upcycling where possible – can make a huge difference.

Sustainability doesn't mean giving up convenience or fun. It just means making choices that benefit your plants, your wallet and the planet all at once. And if you've already made it this far into the book, chances are you're the kind of plant parent who wants to do things better.

So, grow your jungle, but do it right. Because keeping your plants happy shouldn't come at the cost of the planet that made them possible in the first place.

THE ART OF PLANT DISPLAYS
DESIGNING A LIVING MASTERPIECE

Imagine walking into a room and seeing a lush, vibrant, breathing world – plants cascading from shelves like green waterfalls, towering jungle trees standing like ancient guardians, delicate vines creeping over bookcases as if reclaiming lost ruins.

Now, imagine walking into a room with a sad pothos on a shelf and an orchid shoved in a corner like it's being punished. Which world do you want to live in?

That's the difference between arranging plants and creating a plant display.

Your plants are not just décor. They are characters. Some are divas, demanding the spotlight. Some are quiet background players, tying the space together. Some plants are chaotic weirdos, sprawling unpredictably in every direction. The key to an incredible plant display isn't just throwing a bunch of greenery together – it's curating an environment where every plant has its role to play.

So, let's get serious about making your home a masterpiece.

some plants are chaotic weirdos

THE THREE GOLDEN RULES OF PLANT DISPLAYS

Before we dive into different setups, let's lay the foundation for styling your jungle like a pro.

1. LIGHT DICTATES EVERYTHING

Don't put a sun-worshipping succulent in a dark corner unless you want to commit murder. And don't stick a calathea in direct sun unless you want it to wither in slow-motion despair.

Always match the plant's display location to its light needs (see pages 31–37). Your windowsills, shelves and floor spaces aren't just furniture – they're prime real estate.

2. BALANCE AND CONTRAST = INSTANT EYE CANDY

Plants have textures, shapes and heights that need to work together. If everything is bushy and low, it looks flat and unintentional. If everything is upright and stiff, it looks awkwardly formal.

The secret? Layer different shapes and heights:

- **A towering statement plant** – Monstera, bird of paradise.
- **A mid-level bushy companion** – Peace lily, philodendron.
- **A trailing, cascading plant to soften edges** – Pothos, hoya, string of pearls.

Contrast creates visual movement. Mix big, broad leaves with fine, delicate foliage. Pair rigid, upright plants with relaxed, trailing ones. Your jungle should flow.

3. HEALTH OVER AESTHETICS

A display should look stunning and be functional. Don't sacrifice a plant's health just because it looks cool – if it's suffering, the display becomes a slow-motion tragedy.

MASTERING THE ART OF PLANT DISPLAYS

Let's get into the fun stuff – how to create jaw-dropping plant setups that feel intentional, immersive and unique.

THE POWER TRIO: STATEMENT PLANT + SUPPORTING CAST

Want to make your pots look like living art? Use the golden trio: thrillers, fillers and spillers. Your thriller is the star of the show (the Beyoncé of the pot), the fillers are your reliable backing dancers filling in the space and the spillers are the dramatic divas cascading down the sides like they've just fainted from fabulousness. Or think of this as a movie scene. Every plant display should have:

- **The lead role** – A big, bold, eye-catching plant that anchors the scene (monstera, bird of paradise, large dracaena).
- **The supporting cast** – Mid-sized plants that complement the star and create depth (philodendron, fiddle-leaf fig, dieffenbachia).
- **The background extras** – Trailing vines, small ferns and mossy accents that soften the whole look and tie it together.

How to Do It:

- Pick your statement plant first. This is the foundation – your jungle's focal point.
- Choose two to three mid-sized plants that contrast with it in shape, texture or colour.
- Add trailing plants or small accents to fill gaps and complete the look.

Best for: Large corners, feature walls, bookcase setups, side tables.

HANGING GARDENS: ELEVATING YOUR JUNGLE

Not all plants need to be stuck on shelves or floors. Hanging plants create layers and dimension, turning dead space into vibrant green architecture.

How to Do It:

- **Macramé hangers and ceiling hooks** – Create cascading levels by hanging different lengths of plants like pothos, hoyas or string of pearls.
- **Wall-mounted planters** – Attach them to walls for a living plant gallery.
- **Floating shelves and pegboards** – Arrange plants at different heights so they spill over edges in a controlled jungle chaos.

Best for: High ceilings, awkward empty spaces, dramatic window framing.

BOTTOM PLANTING: THE FORGOTTEN LAYER

Most people plonk a big plant in a pot and call it a day – but you can take it further.

How to Do It:

- Pair tall statement trees (fiddle-leaf fig, bird of paradise, large alocasia) with shallow-rooted plants (fittonia, ivy, moss, peperomia) at the base. This fills the empty soil space and creates a natural, layered jungle floor look instead of a sad, bare pot.

Best for: Large feature plants, corner spaces, filling gaps in big pots.

THE 'RECLAIMED RUINS' LOOK: LET PLANTS TAKE OVER

If you want your home to look like nature is winning, this is for you.

How to Do It:

- Encourage vines to creep along bookshelves and walls (attach pothos, *Monstera adansonii* or scindapsus with clear clips).
- Let plants spill over furniture like they own the place (trailing ivy over a dresser, pothos hanging off mirrors).
- Use old objects as planters – vintage teapots, wooden crates or even hollowed-out books.

Best for: Creating that 'lost jungle temple' aesthetic, making your house look like it's slowly being reclaimed by nature.

TERRARIUMS AND MINI ECOSYSTEMS: THE SELF-CONTAINED JUNGLE

Want to create a tiny world of plants inside a glass dome? Welcome to terrarium magic.

How to Do It:

- Use layers – Gravel (for drainage), charcoal (to purify), moss and a rich potting mix.
- Pick plants that love humidity – Ferns, fittonia, moss, small orchids.
- Keep it balanced – Mix heights and textures to create a tiny, thriving landscape.

Best for: Coffee tables, centrepieces, small-space plant lovers.

THE PERSONALITY TEST: WHAT'S YOUR JUNGLE VIBE?

Let's match your display style to your personality.

THE MAXIMALIST JUNGLE LORD

You want your home to look like the Amazon swallowed it whole. Floor-to-ceiling plants, vines covering every surface, zero restraint.

THE MINIMALIST WITH TASTE

You like clean, curated displays – one statement plant per corner, sleek modern pots, no chaos.

THE MAD BOTANIST

You love terrariums, propagations and tiny mini-jungles in glass. You own tweezers specifically for rearranging moss.

THE 'MY HOUSE IS A GREENHOUSE' TYPE

Humidity domes, plant cabinets, full-spectrum grow lights – you're creating a controlled jungle experiment.

FINAL THOUGHTS: YOUR PLANTS DESERVE THE SPOTLIGHT

Your plant collection is alive, growing, evolving – so your displays should do the same. Experiment. Rearrange. Let your jungle take shape organically.

Because at the end of the day? They aren't just houseplants. They're a damn art form.

They aren't just houseplants. They're a damn art form.

LEVEL 6
PLANT CURATOR

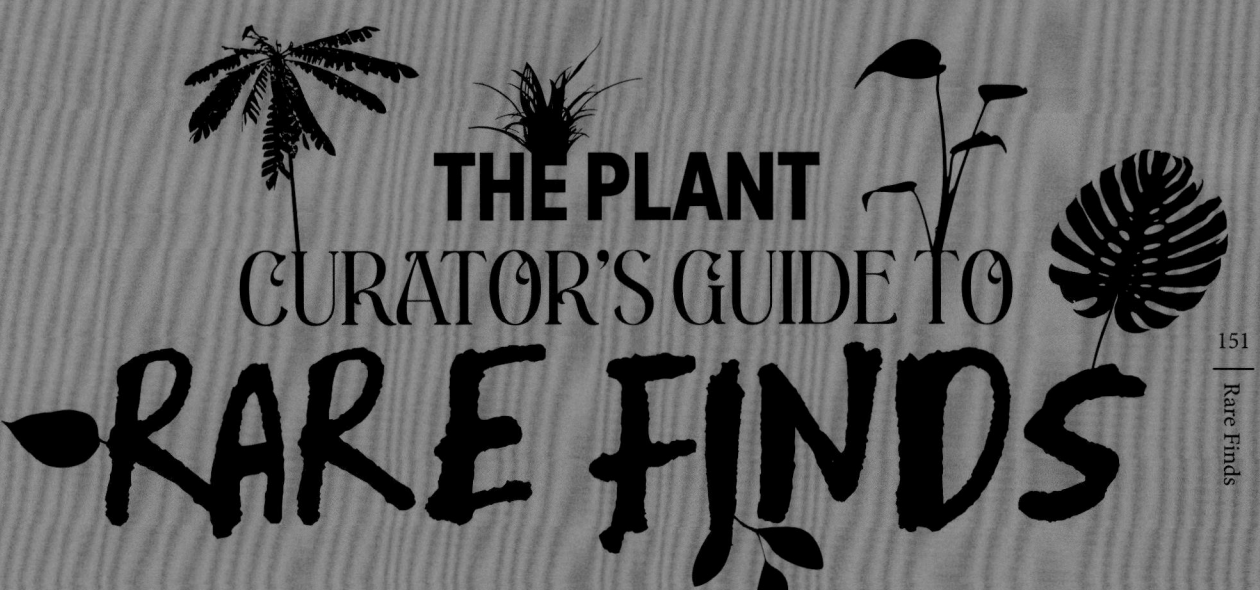

THE PLANT CURATOR'S GUIDE TO RARE FINDS

Welcome to Level 6. You've officially reached plant sensei status. Your pothos and monsteras are thriving, you can spot a pest infestation before it even thinks about showing up, and you've been repotting plants with the ease of a seasoned professional. But now, it's time for the real test – the realm of the rares.

This is where things get serious. No more easy-going, 'I'll survive anything' houseplants. You're entering a world where humidity levels must be precise, light requirements are finicky and mistakes are paid for in crispy leaves and regret. Owning rare plants isn't just about collecting – it's about proving you have the skill, patience and borderline obsession necessary to keep them alive.

So, if you're ready to venture into the high-stakes world of true plant connoisseurs, let's dive in.

WHAT MAKES A PLANT TRULY RARE?

Before you drop a small fortune on that 'exclusive' cutting, let's get real about what actually makes a plant rare. Some plants earn their rarity, while others are just victims of supply-and-demand hype.

A plant is considered truly rare if:

- **It has a hyper-specific natural habitat** – Some plants only grow in tiny pockets of the world, making them difficult (or even illegal) to obtain.

- **It's nearly impossible to propagate quickly** – Plants that take years to mature or are slow to root will always be scarce.

- **It's genetically unstable** – Some rare plants exist only due to mutations or chimeric variegation (an unstable mutation where different types of cells exist within the same plant, causing variegation that can change, revert or be lost over time), making each new growth a gamble (see page 178).

- **It requires precise, hard-to-replicate conditions** – If a plant needs high-altitude mist, constant warmth and pristine water, it's going to stay rare.

And then, of course, there are trendy plants – ones that were once rare but exploded in availability thanks to mass propagation. Remember when *Monstera* 'Albo' was 'impossible to find'? Now, they're everywhere.

THE TRUE HOLY GRAIL OF RARE PLANTS

These plants aren't just rare because they're expensive – they're rare because they're a challenge.

PHILODENDRON SPIRITUS-SANCTI – THE KING OF THE RARE PHILODENDRONS

This plant only exists in a single location in Brazil, with fewer than a hundred in the wild. Elegant, sword-like leaves make it unmistakable, and prices regularly hit thousands.

Care Challenges:

- **It needs 80%+ humidity** – Anything less, and it'll crisp up.

- **Root rot is a death sentence** – If the mix isn't aerated enough, you're finished.

- **It hates being moved** – Slight environmental changes can set it back for months.

Master Tip: Only for serious collectors. If you don't have a perfectly controlled growing environment, you're in for heartbreak.

MONSTERA 'ESQUELETO'

Not to be confused with *Monstera adansonii*, 'Esqueleto' is bigger, rarer and more dramatic. Its leaves develop huge, skeletal fenestrations (extreme holes or slits in leaves where only the main veins remain, with a lace-like or skeletal appearance) that look almost unnatural.

Care Challenges:

- **Needs super bright, indirect light** – Too little, and it grows slow; too much, and it burns.

- **Won't reach its full glory unless climbing** – This is a plant that demands support.

- **Picky about water** – Likes humidity, but hates sitting in wet soil.

Master Tip: Give it a moss pole or trellis to climb if you want to see it reach its full, mind-blowing size. Otherwise, it'll just put out tiny leaves and sulk.

BEGONIA PAVONINA – THE PEACOCK BEGONIA

A literally magical plant. Under normal light, its leaves look like an ordinary, velvety begonia. But hit it with a flashlight or direct beam, and it glows iridescent blue like something out of a sci-fi movie.

Care Challenges:

- **Needs warm, humid conditions (70–80% humidity)** – To show its full colours.
- **It's nearly impossible to find** – If you see one for sale, expect a price that hurts.
- **It hates fluctuations** – Change its environment too fast, and it will drop leaves in protest.

Master Tip: Perfect for a terrarium setup where humidity stays stable. Outside of that? Good luck.

ANTHURIUM FORGETII

This plant makes a statement with its perfectly round, velvet-textured leaves, no sinus (the typical split at the base of anthurium leaves), and stunning silver veining. It's rare because it's painfully slow-growing and high-maintenance.

Care Challenges:

- **Absolutely needs an aroid mix** – Bark, perlite, moss, the works. Anything else, and it'll suffocate.
- **Prone to leaf edge burn** – Without consistent humidity above 70%.
- **Hates being disturbed** – Even repotting can set it back for weeks.

Master Tip: Keep it in a humidity dome or cabinet if you want those velvety leaves to stay pristine.

Monstera deliciosa 'Aurea Variegata'

THE PERSONALITY TEST: WHAT KIND OF RARE PLANT COLLECTOR ARE YOU?

THE RARE HUNTER

You love the thrill of the chase and will spend weeks hunting down a plant before committing to it. Your dream plant? *Philodendron spiritus-sancti*.

THE SCIENTIST

You thrive on experimenting with growth conditions, humidity hacks and propagation strategies. Your perfect match? *Begonia pavonina*, because you love discovering new quirks in plants.

THE AESTHETIC COLLECTOR

Your plants are here to make a statement. You're all about form, texture and contrast, so *Anthurium forgetii* is your must-have.

THE PATIENT GROWER

You don't mind waiting years for a plant to reach its full potential. You're best suited for *Monstera* 'Esqueleto' – because nothing tests patience like slow fenestrations.

THE BRUTAL TRUTH ABOUT RARE PLANTS

If you're getting into rare plants, you need to be prepared for failure. These aren't pothos – you can't neglect them and expect them to bounce back. Some might just … refuse to grow. Some will cost you hundreds and die anyway.

To truly succeed, you need:

- **A controlled environment** – Rare plants thrive best in cabinets, terrariums or grow tents where humidity, light and airflow are perfect.

- **Patience, so much patience** – Some of these plants will test you with agonisingly slow growth.

- **A backup plan.** If a rare plant starts struggling, you need to act fast. Air layering, propagation and emergency setups might be necessary.

FINAL THOUGHTS: THE LAST LEVEL OF PLANT MASTERY

Rare plants are the final test of skill, patience and pure stubborn determination. They demand more, challenge you constantly, and will absolutely punish you for getting things wrong. But when you finally nail the perfect environment and watch that first massive, fenestrated leaf unfurl?

Nothing compares.

So, are you ready to graduate from casual plant parent to true collector? If so – may your humidity stay high, your roots stay aerated and your rare plant wish list never stop growing.

Alocasia micholitziana 'Freydyk' (v)

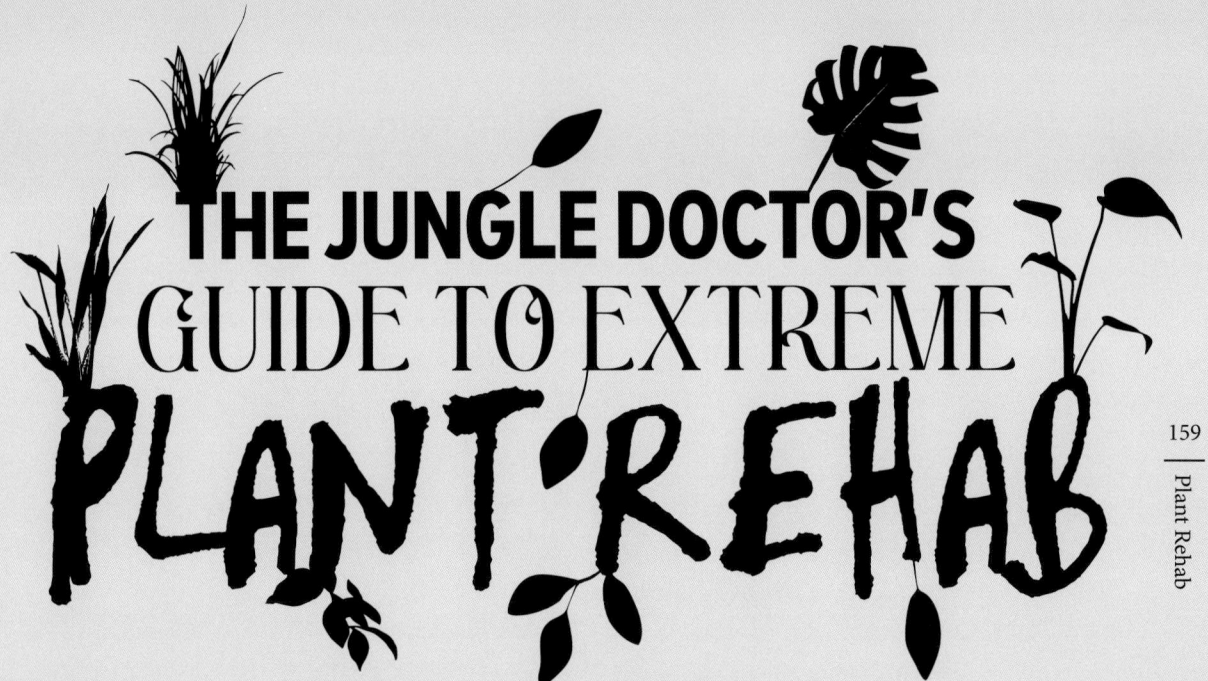

THE JUNGLE DOCTOR'S GUIDE TO EXTREME PLANT REHAB

You're not just a plant parent anymore. You're a plant paramedic. A jungle surgeon. A green-thumbed miracle worker.

By now, you've seen things. Yellowing leaves collapsing like a bad marriage. Stems rotting from the inside out. Plants that look so far gone even a hospice plant collector would give up. But you? You don't throw in the towel. You get the defibrillator. You go to war.

This isn't about tossing a sad-looking plant and replacing it with a fresh one like some heartless capitalist. No. This is about honour. It's about proving that you've got the skill, the patience and the sheer stubbornness to bring them back from the brink.

And sometimes, the difference between life and death is knowing exactly what to do when a plant is circling the drain. So, scrub in, doctor. It's time to save some lives.

> *You're not just a plant parent anymore. You're a plant paramedic.*

STEP ONE: TRIAGE – WHO'S DYING AND WHY?

A plant in critical condition isn't subtle. It's either wilting dramatically, dropping leaves like it's quitting life or rotting from the inside out. The key is diagnosing the crisis before it flatlines.

First, check for a pulse – metaphorically speaking. Is there any sign of life? A single firm root, an unbothered node, a hint of new growth? If yes, then there's hope. If the entire thing is mush, well … get the shovel. Time of death: now.

But if you think you can save it, you need to move fast.

- **Is it drowning?** If the roots are black and soggy and the soil smells like a bog, you're dealing with root rot (see page 130).
- **Is it dying of thirst?** If the soil is cracked like the Sahara and the leaves are crispier than burnt toast, it's severely underwatered (see page 41).
- **Is something attacking it?** Tiny webs? Sticky residue? Chewed-up leaves? Welcome to the world of plant pests – the bastards that never stop ruining lives (see page 68).
- **Has it lost the will to live?** If your variegated plant is pushing out nothing but solid green, congratulations – it's reverting to its boring, energy-efficient ways (see page 178).

Now that you know what's killing it, let's crack open the jungle first-aid kit.

STEP TWO: TOOLS OF THE TRADE – YOUR JUNGLE HOSPITAL KIT

Every good plant rescuer needs the right gear. You don't see surgeons walking into an operation with nothing but vibes. Be prepared.

- **Sharp pruning shears** – Because sometimes you need to amputate with no hesitation and no mercy.
- **Rooting hormone** – For the patients that need a fresh start.
- **Activated charcoal** – Nature's antiseptic. Stops infections, absorbs toxins and smells like survival (see page 49 for more on charcoal).
- **Sphagnum moss** – The ICU for weak plants. Holds moisture, boosts humidity, wraps them in a warm, mossy hug.
- **Perlite and bark mix** – Because dense, suffocating soil is how we got here in the first place.
- **Air stone (for water propagation)** – More oxygen = faster rooting. No one wants stagnant water. That's just death soup.
- **Neem oil and insecticidal soap** – The pest control SWAT team, see page 70.

Got your tools? Let's operate.

Alocasia 'Loco'

STEP THREE: EMERGENCY PROCEDURES

Operation: Root Rot Rescue

This is the most common and deadliest plant emergency. The silent killer. The slow assassin. Your plant looks fine until – BAM! – it collapses like an overwatered house of cards.

You rip the plant out of the pot. The roots? Black, mushy, foul-smelling. You gag. But there's no time for weakness.

Scissors in hand, you start cutting away the infected tissue. You slice until only firm, white roots remain. Then, you dust the survivors with activated charcoal – a plant's version of antiseptic. You repot in light, airy soil, whisper an apology, and promise to be better.

Will It Make It? Time will tell.

Operation: Water Propagation – The Last Resort

The roots are gone. Completely. This isn't surgery – this is an organ transplant.

You take a cutting, just below a node – the plant's last chance at survival. It goes straight into water, but not just any water. Oxygenated, constantly refreshed water.

No air stone? Change the water every three days. Let it stagnate, and you're just watching it rot in slow motion.

Will It Make It? You check every morning like an anxious parent. Come on, little guy, push out those roots. And one day? A tiny white strand emerges. A heartbeat. A pulse. The jungle doctor wins again.

Operation: the Brutal Chop and Restart

Sometimes, a plant is too far gone. Weak stems, leggy growth, entire sections dead on arrival. You can't fix it. But you can reset it.

So, you take a deep breath ... and you chop it down.

Not a trim. Not a tidy-up. A full-blown decapitation.

The plant gasps. You gasp. But soon enough, fresh growth emerges from the cut nodes, stronger than before. Like a phoenix from the ashes, it returns.

Will It Make It? It was never dead – it just needed a fresh start.

STEP FOUR: RECOVERY MODE – KEEPING THE PATIENT ALIVE

The surgery is over, but the aftercare? That's where the real test begins.

- **Humidity is your friend** – A weak plant needs a moisture boost. A covered prop box, a plastic bag, a greenhouse setup – whatever keeps the air moist and the patient stable.

- **Go easy on the water** – Freshly operated plants hate drowning. Water them lightly. Check often.

- **No fertiliser** – You don't feed a patient right after surgery, and you sure as hell don't force-feed a stressed plant. Let it heal first.

- **Monitor** – New growth? Success. Wilting? Adjust. Blackening? Prepare the funeral.

THE JUNGLE DOCTOR'S EMERGENCY ROOM: WHAT KIND OF PLANT MEDIC ARE YOU?

Let's find out what kind of saviour you are when your plant is clinging to life and gasping for chlorophyll.

1. A plant in your care suddenly collapses. What's your first move?

A) Drop everything. Scalpel. Gloves. Activated charcoal. I'm going in.

B) Whisper soothing affirmations while googling 'Why is my plant turning into soup?'

C) Snap a photo and post it to a Facebook group with the caption: 'HELP!!!'

D) Casually move it to the windowsill and hope the sun works some magic.

3. Your favourite plant reverts to green. How do you respond?

A) I cut that bad attitude off and remind it who it used to be.

B) Increase the light, reduce the nitrogen, and speak to it sternly.

C) Cry a little and blame the British weather.

D) Celebrate the return of good ol' reliable green.

2. You find black, mushy roots. What do you do?

A) Surgical precision. Snip. Charcoal. Fresh soil. ICU setup.

B) Panic for 45 seconds, then perform an emergency water propagation.

C) Scream into a pillow, then text your planty mate for moral support.

D) Shrug. 'Nature knows best' and walk away.

4. Your rescue plant finally pushes out a new leaf. What's your reaction?

A) Document the entire process and consider framing the leaf.

B) Happy tears. Maybe even a celebratory cuppa.

C) Tell everyone like you've just had a baby.

D) Nod and say, 'It was inevitable.'

Your Jungle Doctor Diagnosis:

- **The ICU General (Mostly As)** – You are the emergency surgeon of the plant world. Scalpels, shears, humidity tents – you have them all. Plants don't die on your watch. They resurrect.

- **The Passionate Paramedic (Mostly Bs)** – You panic, then you pounce. You might not always know the science, but your heart is in it –and more often than not, you save the day with sheer stubborn love.

- **The Consultative Nurse (Mostly Cs)** – You rely on community care. You're the one flooding the group chat with photos and updates – but you always learn and get better. And your plants love you for it.

- **The Laid-Back Herbalist (Mostly Cs)** – You believe in plant fate. Some live, some die. You'll help if you can, but you don't lose sleep over it. You're chill. Too chill. But hey, some plants dig that.

FINAL THOUGHTS:
EVERY PLANT DESERVES A SECOND CHANCE

Not every plant makes it. Some pull through miraculously. Some fade no matter how hard you fight. That's plant rehab. That's life.

But here's the thing: you don't learn from the perfect plants. You learn from the rescues. The ones that pushed you to observe closer, diagnose faster, and troubleshoot smarter.

Every plant you save makes you a better grower. Every failure teaches you something new.

And if all else fails? Propagate, repot, try again.

Because in this jungle, there's always a second chance.

Now go. Save that plant.

Not every plant makes it

LEVELLING UP LEVELLING UP LEVELLING UP LEVELLING UP

From Jungle Boss to Plant Mystic

You've come far, my friend. From the humble beginnings of overwatering that first pothos to confidently diagnosing nutrient deficiencies with a glance, you've climbed the ranks and earned your stripes.

But now, we're stepping into something deeper. We're about to transcend the tangible and dive into the soul of plants – the unseen, the unexplored, the mind-bending reality of nature's intelligence.

Up until now, you've been learning the how – how to propagate, how to prune, how to fertilise. But what about the why? What if I told you that plants communicate, remember and even respond to the world in ways that science is only just beginning to comprehend? What if I told you that caring for your plants isn't just about keeping them alive, but about forging a connection – one that stretches beyond words, beyond logic, into something ancient and instinctual?

This next section isn't just about plants. It's about you. It's about shifting perspective, unlocking new ways of seeing the world and realising that the jungle you've built isn't just thriving because of what you do – it's thriving because of what you are.

PREPARE TO HAVE YOUR MIND BLOWN

As we step into these next chapters, things are about to get weird – in the best possible way. We're talking about the variegation effect, where we explore why rarity and imperfection make certain plants (and people) special.

We'll uncover the secret underground and the Wood Wide Web, where we find out plants have been gossiping under our feet for millions of years. And we'll take a leap into the science of mutations, because sometimes nature just says, 'Screw it, let's get freaky.'

And if you're ready to fully open your third eye (or at least your green thumb), we'll be diving into the big questions: Do plants remember? Do they feel? Are they, in some strange way, aware of us?

This is where you stop being a plant parent and start becoming a plant philosopher. This is where the jungle becomes a portal.

Breathe deep. Open your mind. Let's go.

PLANT SCIENCE
DEMYSTIFIED UNLOCKING THE JUNGLE CODE

By now, you've moved beyond casual plant care. You don't just water and hope for the best – you know. You've developed that almost supernatural ability to see what your plants need before they even struggle. Yellowing leaf? You're already diagnosing nutrient issues. Leggy growth? You know it's stretching for light before most people even notice.

But here's the thing – understanding plant science isn't just about knowing what your plants need. It's about understanding why they do what they do. Once you crack the code behind how plants function, you stop guessing. You start thinking like a plant – and that's when you become unstoppable.

THE ALCHEMY OF LIGHT: TURNING SUNBEAMS INTO GROWTH

Photosynthesis isn't just a science experiment from school – it's the foundation of life itself. Without it, plants don't grow, leaves don't form, roots don't expand and your indoor jungle would be nothing more than a bunch of sad sticks in pots.

But what's actually happening inside those leaves?

Your plant isn't just sitting there soaking up light like a sunbather on a beach. It's processing energy, converting it into fuel, storing it and distributing it like a well-oiled machine.

1. Chlorophyll absorbs light – Specifically the red and blue wavelengths.

2. That light energy is converted into chemical energy – Producing sugars that fuel every aspect of the plant's survival.

3. The plant moves those sugars around – Sending them where they're needed most, whether it's to push out a new leaf, repair damaged roots or stretch towards the sun.

When your plant thrives, it's because it's getting the perfect balance of light, water and nutrients – the holy trinity of growth.

But when something's off? You'll know.

- **Not enough light?** Your plant will stretch (etiolate) and grow weak, leggy stems.
- **Too much light?** The leaves might burn or bleach, losing their colour as they try to protect themselves.
- **Inconsistent light?** Your plant might start twisting or leaning toward the strongest source, desperately chasing what it needs.

THE UNDERGROUND HIGHWAY: HOW PLANTS 'EAT'

You know that watering is essential, but have you ever considered what's actually happening inside the roots? Your plant isn't just sucking up water – it's absorbing, processing and distributing nutrients like a living pipeline.

Inside every root system, there's a dual transport system keeping the whole plant alive:

- **Xylem** – Think of this like an elevator moving water and nutrients up from the roots to the leaves.
- **Phloem** – This one moves sugars and energy down, feeding new roots, supporting new growth and keeping the plant alive.

When things are working properly, your plant is in growth mode.

But when the system gets disrupted?

- **Underwatering?** The roots struggle to pull up nutrients, leaves start to yellow and growth slows.
- **Overwatering?** The roots suffocate, leading to rot, fungal infections and collapse.
- **Nutrient deficiency?** The plant prioritises survival – new leaves might emerge small and weak, while old leaves yellow and drop off.

And here's where things get really fascinating: **the Wood Wide Web** (see page 185) – a vast underground network of fungi (mycorrhizae) that helps plants exchange nutrients, warn each other of danger and even send food to weaker plants.

Yes. Plants communicate.

HORMONES: THE SECRET MANAGERS OF GROWTH

Every time your plant does anything – grows, flowers, drops leaves, stretches toward light – it's not random. It's chemical warfare inside the plant, where hormones dictate every move.

- **Auxins** – The 'growth director'. These hormones tell stems where to elongate and roots where to expand. This is why plants lean toward light!

- **Cytokinins** – The 'branch manager'. Want bushier growth? These encourage new shoots and side branches.

- **Gibberellins** – The 'size booster.' Responsible for big leaves, longer stems and sudden growth spurts.

- **Abscisic acid** – The 'survival mode switch'. Triggers leaf drop, dormancy and other stress responses.

- **Ethylene** – The 'release signal'. Tells plants to drop leaves, ripen fruit or kill off weak parts.

When you pinch back a plant to encourage bushier growth, you're literally manipulating its hormone balance. When you repot and trim roots, you trigger a surge of growth hormones.

Once you understand how these natural chemicals work, you'll know exactly how to shape and train your plants with precision.

Cast-iron plant

FINAL THOUGHTS: SCIENCE IS YOUR SUPERPOWER

Plant science isn't just a bunch of boring facts – it's the key to mastering plant care at the highest level.

- If you understand how light fuels a plant – You'll never struggle with leggy growth again.
- If you understand how nutrients move through roots – You'll never panic over yellowing leaves.
- If you understand plant hormones – You'll manipulate growth like a true jungle architect.

Once you start thinking like a plant – adjusting, experimenting, adapting – you'll realise you've unlocked the highest level of plant mastery.

And from here? There's no limit to what you can grow.

There's no limit to what you can grow

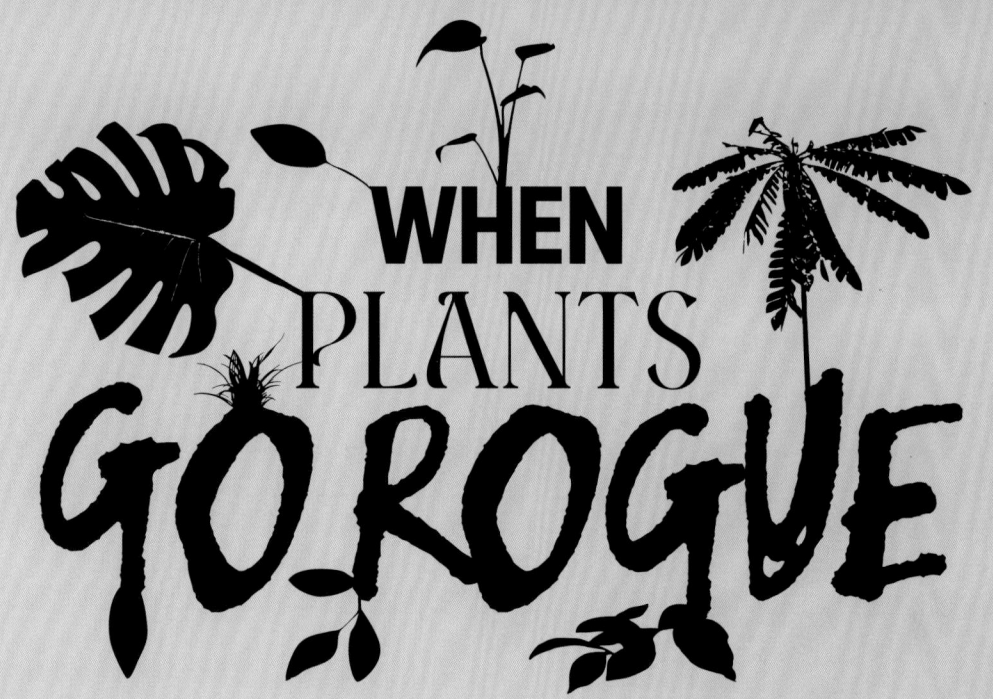

When Plants Go Rogue

Nature is not perfect. It never has been. It doesn't create order – it creates chaos, and then it sits back and watches what happens. Every single plant mutation – every twisted leaf, every splash of white, every streak of pink – is nature breaking its own rules.

And let's be honest, we love a good rule-breaker.

Variegation, that holy grail of the plant world, is nothing more than a glitch in the system. A genetic hiccup that leaves a plant partially blind to the sun, struggling to produce enough energy, yet somehow looking like an ethereal, otherworldly masterpiece in the process. It's rare, it's unstable, and it makes plant collectors lose their minds.

But variegation is only one kind of mutation. Plants mutate all the time. Sometimes, the results are spectacular – new species, new growth forms, plants that look like they belong in an alien landscape. Other times? It's a genetic dead-end, a plant too weak to survive on its own.

This is the underground world of plant mutations – the beautiful accidents, the evolutionary gambles and the plants that refuse to follow the rules.

VARIEGATION: NATURE'S HAPPY ACCIDENT

To the untrained eye, variegation looks like aesthetic perfection. But to the plant? It's a handicap.

Chlorophyll is the lifeblood of plants – the molecule that traps sunlight and turns it into energy. Lose patches of it, and suddenly, you've got a high-maintenance diva on your hands. Less energy production means slower growth, weaker stems and a plant that constantly needs you to babysit its light levels.

But we love it anyway. Why? Because imperfection is mesmerising.

A full-green monstera is beautiful. But a *Monstera* 'Albo'? That's art. A splash of creamy white running through the leaf like a lightning strike, a pattern so unique that no two leaves will ever be the same – that's the kind of mutation that turns a plant into a legend.

But not all variegation is created equal. Some plants will hold onto their unique patterns forever, while others? They're constantly teetering on the edge of losing it all.

The Variegation Spectrum: Unpredictable, Untamed, Unruly

Some plants embrace their mutations like a tattooed rebel who refuses to conform. Others try to claw their way back to normalcy the moment they get a chance.

Take the *Philodendron* 'Pink Princess'. One day, it's producing bright pink leaves that look like they've been airbrushed by a Renaissance artist. The next? Leaves are a solid green. And once a 'Pink Princess' starts reverting, you have a small window to cut away the green and beg it to stay pink, or it's gone forever.

Then you have plants like the *Scindapsus pictus*, where the variegation is written into its very DNA, hardcoded into its genetics like an unchangeable destiny. It doesn't matter if you propagate it, stress it out or throw it in the darkest corner of your house – it will always come back with that same silver sheen.

And let's not forget the frauds – plants that develop pale streaks not because they're rare, but because they're stressed out. A calathea that looks washed out under bad lighting, an alocasia that gets pale after a cold spell – these are not 'new variegated' forms. They're just plants having a bad day.

BEYOND VARIEGATION: WHEN PLANTS GET FREAKY

Variegation might be the celebrity mutation, but it's only one type of botanical rebellion. Sometimes, plants don't just change their colour – they change their entire identity.

Twisted Leaves and Warped Forms

Some plants decide that regular leaves are boring.

The *Monstera* 'Burle Marx Flame' takes its fenestrations to the extreme, shredding each leaf until it looks like an impossibly intricate lace pattern, something so wild it feels like it shouldn't exist.

The *Philodendron tortum* barely even looks like a philodendron anymore – its leaves are thin, skeletal, almost alien. It's as if nature tried to draw a fern from memory and got it completely wrong.

These aren't just mutations. They're new blueprints, new ideas, plants literally experimenting on themselves to see what else is possible.

Growth Habit Mutations: the Rebels That Refuse to Grow Normally

Some plants? They refuse to follow any of the usual rules.

Ever seen a pothos that doesn't trail? A vining plant that decides it's going to stand upright like a tree? Some pothos varieties, through a random genetic switch-up, start growing like bushes instead of vines, rewriting the entire playbook of how they're supposed to behave.

Or take the *Syngonium* 'Ice Frost', which naturally grows in a more compact, structured shape compared to its sprawling, leggy cousins.

It's like watching an indoor jungle revolt – plants flipping the script on their own growth patterns, deciding they don't want to be vines, climbers or rosettes anymore. They want to be something else.

Tissue Culture Mutations: the Lab-Created Freaks

Not all mutations happen in the wild. Some? We made them.

Tissue culture – the process of cloning plants in a lab – has given us some of the most famous houseplants on Earth.

Take the *Monstera* 'Thai Constellation' – a plant so stunning that scientists had to step in and start mass-producing it. But here's the catch: tissue-cultured plants tend to be weaker. They grow slower, they demand more care and they often come with unexpected mutations.

Lab-grown beauty isn't always easy.

CARING FOR ROGUE PLANTS: KEEPING THE MUTATIONS ALIVE

Own a variegated or mutated plant? Congratulations – you now have a high-maintenance diva on your hands.

Light is everything. Too little, and they'll start pushing out solid green leaves like they're trying to escape their own mutation. Too much? Sunburn. There's no middle ground with these guys.

Reverting? Cut back to the last variegated node. No mercy. If you hesitate, your plant will go full green and never look back.

And stress? Avoid it like the plague. Unstable mutations can disappear if the plant feels threatened. No sudden changes, no experimental care routines – keep things steady.

Monstera deliciosa 'Albo Variegata'

FINAL THOUGHTS: BEAUTY COMES AT A COST

Mutations are nature's wild experiments – sometimes they create icons, sometimes they self-destruct and sometimes they change the plant world forever.

Owning a variegated or mutated plant isn't just about aesthetics – it's about preserving a moment of botanical rebellion. It's about nurturing something that, by all logic, shouldn't exist – but does.

And that's the magic of it.

If you're up for the challenge, these plants will reward you with some of the most jaw-dropping, one-of-a-kind foliage you'll ever see. But if you're not?

Stick to the solid greens. They'll never let you down.

Mutations are nature's wild experiments

THE SECRET UNDERGROUND LIFE BENEATH THE POT

If you think the real action in your plant's life is happening above the soil, let me stop you right there. Beneath every thriving monstera, every climbing philodendron and every anthurium pushing out a perfect, glossy leaf, there is an entire underground universe – one you never see, but one that holds all the power.

This is the Underground Jungle.

And just like the real jungle, it's chaotic, intricate, full of secret networks, unspoken alliances and power struggles. It's not just a place where roots sit quietly in soil, waiting for water. It's a living, breathing ecosystem.

But here's the crazy part – plants aren't just living in it. They're talking in it. They're trading in it. They're helping (or sabotaging) each other in it.

Your plant's roots aren't just sucking up nutrients like a straw in a smoothie. They're sending messages, making deals and even bribing fungi to work for them.

Let's crack open the pot and see what's really going on down there.

THE WOOD WIDE WEB

We love a good internet conspiracy, but this one's real. The Wood Wide Web isn't some poetic nonsense – it's a full-blown, scientifically proven phenomenon first brought to light by Dr. Suzanne Simard, a badass forest ecologist who spent years digging (literally) into how plants and fungi form vast underground communication networks.

What she discovered? Plants don't just grow in soil. They communicate through it.

Imagine an ancient tree in the middle of a rainforest, towering above the rest, with a root system deep enough to tap into underground water reservoirs. Next to it? A tiny sapling, barely clinging to life, its roots too weak to reach the good stuff.

In a standard 'every plant for itself' world, that sapling would die trying. But through the Wood Wide Web, the mother tree – let's call her Big Mama Monstera – can send resources to that struggling seedling.

Not out of kindness. Not out of love.

But because the health of the forest depends on the whole network surviving. The trees, the undergrowth, the seedlings, the fungi – they're all connected.

And fungi? They're the ones running the show.

Their tiny, thread-like structures – called mycorrhizae – act as fibre-optic cables, linking plant roots together into one giant underground data centre. They are the secret life support system of the Underground Jungle.

These fungi form actual partnerships with plant roots, merging with them on a cellular level and working as nutrient couriers – in exchange for a little sugar.

Yep, plants literally pay fungi in sugar to work for them.

Fungi, in return, deliver phosphorus, nitrogen and other hard-to-reach nutrients straight to the plant's roots.

It's like hiring a personal assistant for your plant's root system.

HOW IT WORKS: THE SECRET TRADE DEALS BENEATH YOUR FEET

So, let's break this down:

- **Resource sharing** – Older, established plants send nutrients and water to weaker or younger plants, keeping the entire ecosystem strong.

- **Warning signals** – When a plant detects an attack – like an insect invasion or a disease – it can warn its neighbours, triggering them to start producing their own defences before the threat arrives.

- **Nutrient redistribution** – If one plant is struggling, others might lend a hand (or a root, in this case) by sharing phosphorus, nitrogen and sugars through the fungal network.

Basically, it's a stock market, a military intelligence service and a community support group – all happening below ground.

Just like the real jungle, it's chaotic, intricate, full of secret networks

YOUR HOUSEPLANTS ARE DOING THIS TOO

Now, this isn't just some deep forest magic – it happens inside your plant pots too.

If you're growing multiple plants in the same soil (or even near each other), their roots can connect through fungal partners, allowing them to share resources, send chemical warnings and even redistribute nutrients based on who needs them most.

But not every plant plays fair.

THE UNDERGROUND HUSTLERS: PLANTS THAT CHEAT THE SYSTEM

Just like the internet has hackers and scammers, the fungal network has freeloaders.

Some plants don't contribute anything back into the system – they steal.

Take orchids. Certain orchids don't even bother making their own food when they're young. They hijack the fungal network, siphoning nutrients away from others until they've grown strong enough to photosynthesise on their own.

Then there's the infamous ghost orchid (*Dendrophylax lindenii*) – a plant that doesn't even have leaves. Instead of bothering with photosynthesis, it just leeches off the underground network like a plant vampire.

Even in your own home, some plants are hungrier than others. Ever noticed how some plants explode with growth while others struggle in the same soil mix? Some are just better at making fungal deals than others.

If your monstera is thriving while your calathea is sulking, now you know why.

BRINGING THE UNDERGROUND JUNGLE TO YOUR PLANTS

Now that you know what's really going on beneath the soil, how do you make sure your houseplants aren't just surviving – but thriving?

- **First rule: stop using lifeless soil** – Bagged potting mixes are often sterile – meaning they're about as lively as a brick. If you want the underground jungle to flourish, you need to introduce life into the mix.

Best way? Worm castings, compost and mycorrhizal inoculants. These jumpstart microbial activity and give plants the underground allies they need.

- **Second rule: encourage root exploration** – Roots love space, oxygen and a little resistance. Ever wondered why plants in chunky, airy mixes tend to grow bigger, faster and stronger? It's because their roots are getting plenty of air and stimulation, which triggers more growth.

Best way? Go for a mix with perlite, pine bark and coco coir to keep those roots moving.

- **Final rule: water wisely** – A thriving underground ecosystem needs balance. Too much water? The fungi drown. Too little? They go dormant.

Best way? Keep the soil consistently moist, but never soggy, to maintain the best conditions for root-fungal cooperation.

not every plant plays fair

FINAL THOUGHTS: THE SECRET BENEATH THE SOIL

You didn't just buy a plant.

You brought home an entire ecosystem.

Every time you water, every time you repot, every time you watch a new leaf unfurl, there's an entire underground world working tirelessly to make it happen.

And the more you respect what's happening beneath the surface, the more you can create a thriving, self-sustaining jungle in your home.

So, next time you admire your monstera's latest leaf or wonder why your philodendron is pushing out new growth so fast – remember, it's not just what you're doing, it's what's happening underground.

Philodendron gloriosum

THE ANATOMY OF GROWTH

Plants are architects, engineers and builders – but instead of bricks and steel, they're working with sunlight, water and whatever scraps of nutrients they can scavenge from their environment. No planning permission. No instruction manual. Just raw instinct, telling them when to reach for the sky, when to branch out and when to sit tight and focus on their roots.

And let's be real – plants don't always take the most elegant approach to growth. You give them a shelf, they'll lunge towards the nearest window like a drunk trying to find the exit. Leave them unchecked, and they'll climb your furniture, strangle your other plants or spill onto the floor like they own the place.

But this madness? It's not random. It's strategy. Plants are out there playing 4D chess, shaping themselves around whatever environment they find themselves in. And once you understand the mechanics behind it, you can work with them instead of against them.

PLANTS DON'T JUST GROW – THEY SCHEME

Unlike humans, who just expand in every direction if we eat too much pizza, plants don't waste energy on mindless growth. Every new leaf, every root extension, every ridiculous vine reaching for the ceiling is intentional.

At the heart of this operation are meristems – tiny cellular powerhouses that act like construction sites.

At the tips of stems and roots, you've got the apical meristems – the reason your monstera is suddenly eyeballing your ceiling and your pothos won't stay in its damn pot. These are the zones of length growth, and they are relentless.

Then there are lateral meristems, the thickening agents. These turn spindly stems into chunky, structural supports. If your once-flimsy fiddle-leaf fig suddenly looks like it could survive a hurricane, you've got lateral meristems to thank.

Prune the apical meristem? The plant redirects its energy to lateral meristems, pushing out more side shoots instead of reaching upward. Leave it alone? It'll just keep climbing until it runs out of space – or your patience.

This is why pruning is not just about aesthetics – it's about strategy. You're literally telling your plant where to grow.

WATER: THE SECRET GROWTH INGREDIENT

Let's clear something up – new plant cells start tiny, lifeless and useless. They don't actually become plant material until they absorb water and stretch out. Imagine filling up a balloon – that's what water does to every new cell.

And this is where so many people go wrong. Too little water? The plant can't inflate those cells properly, so growth slows to a crawl. Too much water? The roots suffocate, and growth stops dead.

If your plant hasn't done anything in months, check your watering routine before you start throwing fancy fertilisers at it. You can pump it full of nutrients all you want, but if it doesn't have the hydration to stretch those new cells? Nothing's happening.

LIGHT: THE MASTER PUPPETEER

If plants had eyes, they'd be obsessed with light. It tells them where to grow, how fast to grow, and even what shape to take. No light? No photosynthesis. No photosynthesis? No energy. No energy? Congratulations, you've got yourself a decorative twig.

This is why plants lean dramatically toward windows – it's phototropism in action. They're not just reaching for the light; they're actively reshaping themselves to chase it.

Ever noticed that a plant left in the same position for too long starts growing lopsided? That's auxin – a sneaky little hormone that builds up on the shady side of the plant, elongating those cells and bending the whole thing toward the light.

Solution? Quarter turn. Every week. Otherwise, you'll wake up one morning to find your plant leaning so far forward it looks like it's trying to escape.

But too much direct light? Different disaster. Most houseplants evolved under dense canopies, meaning full sun is about as welcome as a sunbed with no sunscreen. Scorched leaves, faded colours, crispy edges – your plant is burning alive. If it could scream, it would.

ROOTS: THE SILENT COMMAND CENTRE

What's happening above the soil is only half the story. The real power move? It's happening below the surface.

Roots aren't just anchors – they're nutrient hunters, water absorbers and chemical signallers, working non-stop to keep the whole operation running. They come in two main types:

- **Taproots** – The deep divers. Think of a carrot – one massive root plunging straight down. These plants hate being in shallow pots.
- **Fibrous roots** – The spreaders. These roots fan out wide, grabbing everything they can. They love wide, shallow containers where they can branch out properly.

Overwatering? That's public enemy number one for roots. They don't just need water – they need oxygen too. Drown them, and they suffocate. The plant shuts down, growth stops and you're left wondering why your leafy baby suddenly looks like it needs life support.

If you've ever yanked a dead plant from its pot and been hit with the smell of swampy death, congrats – you've just experienced root rot.

LEAVES: THE SOLAR PANELS OF THE PLANT WORLD

If roots are the underground workers, leaves are the power stations, cranking out energy through photosynthesis (see page 172). They're packed with tiny chloroplasts, which absorb light, convert it into sugar and power the whole damn operation.

But leaves do more than just collect energy – they also control water release through stomata. These microscopic pores open and close to let in carbon dioxide, but they also lose water in the process.

Too much water loss? Hello, crispy brown edges.

Too little water intake? Drooping, wilting, sad-looking leaves.

And let's talk about variegated plants for a second. Those gorgeous white patches? Yeah, they don't contain chlorophyll, which means they can't photosynthesise. That's why variegated plants grow slower – they're operating at half capacity.

Want them to keep their colour? Give them more light. No light = the green parts start taking over to compensate.

PLANTS THAT NEVER STOP GROWING

Some plants have built-in limits – they grow to a certain size, then stop. Others? They keep going forever if the conditions are right.

That's why pothos and ivy will take over your entire house if you let them. These indeterminate growers have no stop button – unless you decide to step in.

So, if you want to keep things under control, you need to prune. Otherwise, you'll come home one day to find your plant has started annexing other furniture.

> *If roots are the underground workers, leaves are the power stations*

FINAL THOUGHTS: GROWTH IS A STRATEGY, NOT A COINCIDENCE

Your plants aren't just growing – they're engineering their own future.

- Want a bushier plant? Prune it (see page 119).
- Want bigger leaves? Sort out your watering and light.
- Want it to stop leaning like a drunk at closing time? Rotate it.

Once you understand how a plant builds itself, you stop guessing and start shaping. Every new shoot, every fresh root, every unfurling leaf – it's all part of a bigger strategy.

And now? You're in control of that strategy.

Haworthiopsis fasciata

HOW WE MADE HOUSEPLANTS BEHAVE (SORT OF)

Houseplants sit there all prim and proper, perched on shelves, trailing elegantly from macramé hangers, making you feel like you've got your life together. But don't let their polite, potted existence fool you. These leafy housemates weren't always so well-mannered.

Every single one of them came from the wild – climbing trees in humid jungles, stretching across vast deserts or clinging to the cracks of remote mountain cliffs. And yet, here they are, trapped in your living room, adjusting to your sporadic watering schedule, surviving on whatever sunlight filters through your IKEA blinds.

How the hell did that happen? How did we go from untamed, survivalist plants to needy fiddle-leaf figs that throw tantrums when moved two inches to the left?

Well, my friend, buckle up – because the story of how we tamed the wild is nothing short of ridiculous.

THE FIRST PLANT PARENTS: WHEN NATURE MOVED INDOORS

Once upon a time, plants didn't live indoors. Shocking, I know. They had no pots, no curated aesthetic, no dedicated Instagram pages. They were just out there, doing their thing, until humans decided to get involved.

The ancient Egyptians were some of the first plant parents, growing palms and papyrus in courtyard gardens over 4,000 years ago. Meanwhile, the Chinese dynasties took things to the next level, miniaturising trees into bonsai because, apparently, nature wasn't artistic enough for them.

The Romans? They were draping ivy and laurels around their villas, flexing on their neighbours with lavish indoor gardens. And then came the Victorians, who turned plant collecting into an extreme sport, stuffing their homes with ferns, orchids and anything that would survive in their dimly lit, over-decorated parlours.

Fast forward to today, and houseplants are a global obsession. We've taken plants that were built for untamed wilderness and forced them to survive in artificially heated apartments, on bookshelves, next to Wi-Fi routers, with a cat chewing on their leaves.

And somehow, they've adapted. Mostly.

HOW WE CHANGED HOUSEPLANTS (AND HOW THEY CHANGED US)

Domestication isn't just for dogs and cats. Over centuries, we've shaped plants to fit our homes, breeding them to be smaller, hardier and – let's be honest – prettier. But no matter how much we've modified them, they still carry the instincts of their wild ancestors.

Shrinking for small spaces

Wild plants grow big and unruly. But we don't all live in rainforest-sized homes, so breeders have spent years selecting for compact growth.

Ever wondered why your ZZ plant is practically indestructible? That's because in the wild, its ancestors grew tough to survive droughts. We just miniaturised the attitude and made it perfect for people who forget to water their plants (yes, I see you).

Adapting to dimmer conditions

Most wild plants grow in bright, open landscapes – but indoors? Not so much. Over time, we selected species that could tolerate shade, making them ideal for our gloomy British winters and rented flats with one decent window.

Snake plants, pothos, peace lilies – these guys thrive in places so dark a vampire would struggle. Not because they prefer it, but because they're built for survival.

Changing for the aesthetic

Nature is cool, but humans can't help themselves – we wanted more variegation, more pink, more drama. So, we bred plants for colour, shape and sheer vibe.

That stunning *Monstera* 'Thai Constellation' you've been eyeing? Not found in the wild. It was created in a lab through tissue culture. The Pink Princess philodendron? Another human-engineered masterpiece, selectively bred for those coveted blush-toned splashes.

Messing with seasonal cycles

In the wild, plants follow a rhythm – growing in the right season, resting in the off-season. But we threw that whole concept out the window.

Indoor plants now live in a world of artificial lighting and central heating, where winter doesn't feel like winter, and summer might as well be a rumour. As a result, some plants never stop growing, while others (like alocasias) still go dormant anyway, confused as hell.

> Nature is cool, but humans can't help themselves

Monstera 'Thai Constellation'

THE WILD SIDE: TRAITS THAT STILL PERSIST

But for all our efforts, some habits die hard. You might think you've tamed your houseplant, but it's still got jungle instincts tucked into its DNA.

Take aerial roots, for example. You didn't ask for them, you probably don't want them, but here they are – snaking out of your monstera like they're planning an escape. That's because in the wild, those roots latch onto tree trunks, helping the plant climb towards the light. In your living room? They're just … hanging around, doing nothing except making your plant look like it's considering a second career as a horror movie prop.

Then there's the stubborn independence of succulents. These plants hoard water like they're expecting the next apocalpse because in their natural desert homes, rain is rare and unpredictable. The result? They're really bad at letting go, holding onto every drop you give them – even when it's too much. Overwater them, and instead of drinking responsibly, they just implode, rotting from the inside out like some tragic Greek tragedy.

And let's not forget dormancy. You think your plant is thriving, you're giving it perfect care and suddenly – it stops. Growth? Nada. New leaves? Nope. You start questioning everything, but your plant? It's just obeying the ancient rhythms of nature, shutting down for a seasonal nap because, deep down, it still believes it's out in the wild.

HOW HOUSEPLANTS CHANGED US

While we were busy domesticating plants, they were secretly domesticating us too.

They've dictated design trends for centuries, from the fern-filled homes of the Victorians to today's obsession with making your flat look like a jungle.

They've hacked our brains, tricking us into caring for them because science says tending to plants reduces stress, improves focus and generally makes us better humans.

And now? They're pushing technology forward – smart pots, self-watering systems, even plants that change colour when air quality declines. One day, your pothos might be able to text you when it's thirsty.

> You might think you've tamed your houseplant, but it's still got jungle instincts tucked into its DNA

FINAL THOUGHTS: TAMING THE WILD, BUT KEEPING IT ALIVE

Houseplants may look cute and obedient in their little pots, but every single one still carries the DNA of its wild ancestors.

Your fiddle-leaf fig? Its ancestors were towering rainforest giants. Your peace lily? It evolved in swampy jungles, not on a coffee table. And that *Monstera* 'Albo' you just spent a fortune on? It's literally a genetic anomaly humans decided to propagate.

So, next time your monstera tries to take over the room, or your fern throws a fit about humidity, just remember – you didn't just bring a plant indoors.

You brought a piece of the wild. And it's doing its best to behave – even if it still dreams of climbing trees, sprawling across a jungle floor or basking under the unfiltered sun.

Tamed? Sort of. Still wild at heart? Always.

Monstera deliciosa 'Albo Variegata'

PLANT SENTIENCE

ARE THEY MORE ALIVE THAN WE THINK?

A plant sits still. No face. No voice. No movement. It doesn't wince when you prune it. It doesn't whimper when it's thirsty. It doesn't cry when it's dying. And because of that, we've always assumed it's just … there. A thing. Alive, yes, but not aware. Not in any way that matters.

But what if we've been wrong? What if plants are not just growing, not just reacting, but actually experiencing the world in a way we've never considered?

For centuries, humans have drawn a hard line between plants and animals, between awareness and mere existence. Plants, we decided, don't think, they don't feel, they don't know anything at all. But what if they do?

Not in the way we do. Not with thoughts, not with emotions, not with a brain quietly spinning through anxieties about whether their monstera cuttings will root. But in their own way. A way that science is only just beginning to understand.

It's an unsettling thought, isn't it? The idea that every time you walk past your plants, they might – on some level – know you're there.

DO PLANTS KNOW WHAT'S HAPPENING TO THEM?

Imagine you're a plant. Your world isn't silent or still. It's rich with sensation, an unending flood of information that tells you everything you need to survive.

You know where the light is. You track it. You shift your leaves, adjusting angle by angle, chasing the sun like a slow-motion dance no one else can see.

You feel the moisture in the air. You pull water from the soil, rationing every drop when the air grows dry.

You sense when something brushes against you. If it's a friendly touch – like a nearby tree – you wrap around it, climbing higher. If it's a threat – like an insect – you flood your leaves with bitter chemicals, warning the predator off before it even takes a bite.

It's easy to dismiss this as instinct. A programmed response. But that raises a question – how do they know the difference between what matters and what doesn't?

Take the *Neptunia oleracea*, a water-loving relative of the sensitive plant (*Mimosa pudica*). Much like its famous cousin, its leaves fold up when touched. But here's where it gets interesting – it responds faster to strong touches and slower to light, harmless disturbances. It's not just reacting – it's evaluating.

Or consider the Cape sundew (*Drosera capensis*) – a carnivorous plant that traps insects with sticky, glistening tentacles. When a struggling bug lands, the sundew doesn't immediately wrap around it. It waits. It distinguishes between prey and debris, only moving if the struggling continues.

And what about trees? *Acacia tortilis*, an African thorn tree, has a built-in chemical defence system. When a giraffe starts munching on its leaves, the tree quickly pumps tannins into its foliage, making them bitter and unpalatable. But it doesn't stop there – it also releases airborne distress signals that warn nearby acacias, triggering them to do the same before they're even touched.

An orchid knows the seasons. It doesn't bloom just because it's warm – it remembers how long the cold lasted and decides whether it's safe to flower.

A philodendron growing in deep shade doesn't just sit there, waiting for light to reach it. It sends out vines, testing different directions, looking for something to climb. It chooses the best path. It decides where to go.

A ficus tree, when cut back too aggressively, will redirect its energy, focusing on survival. It won't just sprout leaves at random – it knows where the damage is and responds accordingly.

Does that sound like a passive, mindless organism to you?

THE WEIRD WAYS PLANTS STORE MEMORY

Alright, so we've established that plants remember. But how? They don't have a brain or a nervous system, so where is this memory hiding? Turns out, plants are wired differently – literally.

Instead of a brain, plants send signals through their bodies in completely alien ways.

First up, electrical signals. Sounds human, right? Well, plants use them too. When something happens – say, a leaf gets nibbled on – an electrical pulse shoots through the plant, warning other areas to brace for impact.

This is how a plant under attack can ramp up its defences before the next bite even happens.

Then there are calcium waves, which are basically a plant's emergency broadcast system. Imagine something stressful happens – drought, damage, temperature drop. The plant sends out waves of calcium through its cells, spreading the news like wildfire. The next time the same stress happens? It reacts faster.

And then we get to plant hormones, the real masterminds. When a plant experiences stress, it releases chemical signals that help it survive next time. A plant that barely survived a dry spell will close its stomata faster next time water runs low. One that got chomped by bugs last season? It toughens up its leaves for round two.

But the craziest thing? Some plants don't just learn for themselves – they pass the knowledge down.

This is where things get truly wild.

MEMORY THAT OUTLIVES THE PLANT

Imagine if your great-grandparents lived through a drought and, because of that, you were born with the ability to survive longer without water. Sounds insane, right? But plants actually do this.

Through a process called epigenetics, plants alter the way their genes are expressed based on past experiences.

A plant that endures a brutal pest attack doesn't just learn to defend itself – it can pass stronger, more resilient traits down to its offspring. A seed from a drought-stricken plant might grow into a more drought-tolerant version of itself – before it's ever been thirsty.

Plants aren't just surviving – they're evolving in real-time.

So, the next time someone says, 'It's just a plant,' feel free to hit them with this knowledge bomb.

Jade plant

THE UNDERGROUND NETWORK: A SILENT INTELLIGENCE?

And it gets weirder. Because plants aren't just aware of their own existence – they communicate.

Not with words, but with chemicals, with electrical signals, with the vast underground network of fungi otherwise known as the Wood Wide Web (see page 185).

In tropical rainforests, massive mother trees send nutrients to saplings through their roots. They favour their own offspring, feeding them more than unrelated trees.

In dense jungles, plants coordinate defences. One gets attacked, the others react. It's not a coincidence – it's an exchange of information.

Even in your own home, right now, your plants may be subtly responding to each other. A chemical shift in one can trigger changes in another. A stress response in one can influence the health of its neighbours.

This isn't science fiction. This isn't some mystical, tree-hugger fantasy. This is proven, studied, real-life plant behaviour.

So, if plants can sense, communicate and even anticipate threats ... what does that make them?

ARE PLANTS INTELLIGENT?

Now, the idea of plant intelligence is controversial. Scientists fight over this one like it's the heavyweight championship of botany.

But let's look at the facts:

- **Plants communicate** – Some send chemical messages through the air, warning their neighbours about incoming pests.
- **They solve problems** – Vines like philodendrons actively search for things to climb and change direction if they don't find one.
- **They make decisions** – A plant given multiple light sources will choose the best one – not just guess.

Critics argue that these are just automatic responses, that plants aren't really thinking – they're just running on instinct. But the line between instinct and intelligence starts to blur when a plant learns, remembers and adapts to new situations.

They don't have thoughts. They don't have emotions. But they damn well react to the world in ways that suggest something deeper is going on.

This isn't science fiction

FINAL THOUGHTS: RETHINKING WHAT IT MEANS TO BE ALIVE

For centuries, we've measured intelligence by how similar something is to us. If it doesn't have a brain, it can't think. If it doesn't have a face, it can't feel. If it doesn't move, it isn't aware.

But plants are challenging all of that.

They exist on their own terms, in a way we're only just starting to understand. They are active participants in their world, not passive objects. They sense, respond and adapt.

And that means we have two choices.

We can keep pretending plants are just decoration, nice little green things to brighten up a room. Or we can start seeing them for what they really are.

Because next time you brush your hand over a leaf, or move a plant into better light or wonder why your monstera's aerial roots seem determined to escape their pot – stop and think.

Maybe it's not just growing.

Maybe it's aware.

Maybe, in its own strange, silent way …

It's watching you too.

Congratulations, Jungle Guru!

Well, look at you. Standing at the top of the mountain, surveying your kingdom – a lush, thriving, oxygen-pumping testament to your newfound mastery. You've conquered the chaos of plant care, outwitted pests, nurtured life from cuttings and cracked the code behind what makes plants grow, thrive and sometimes act like dramatic little divas.

This isn't just a collection of potted greenery anymore. This is your jungle. Your empire. Your legacy.

You've levelled up – for good.

Think back to when you first cracked open this book. Maybe you were sweating over a sad, crispy fern, wondering where it all went wrong. Maybe you were a casual collector, looking to take things up a notch. Or maybe you were already knee-deep in soil but wanted to understand the science behind the madness.

Wherever you started, you're not that person anymore.

Now? You don't just own plants – you understand them.

- You can read leaves like a fortune teller.
- You know when to water, when to wait and when to intervene like a jungle doctor.
- You can propagate, prune, repot and even bend nature to your will.

That's power. That's wisdom. That's the mark of a true Jungle Boss.

And the best part? This is just the beginning.

A BOOK THAT GROWS WITH YOU

This isn't a book you read once and forget. It's a living, breathing manual – one that will be here whenever you need it. Got a new plant? Flip back and brush up on care. Need a laugh after a tragic overwatering incident? I got you.

This book isn't just mine anymore. It's yours.

And speaking of that, let me just say: I'm ridiculously proud of you. Writing this was a labour of love (and mild insanity), but knowing that you've laughed, learnt and stuck with me through every chapter? That means everything.

This book isn't just mine anymore. It's yours.

FINAL THOUGHTS: WHAT PLANTS HAVE TAUGHT YOU

Plants don't just sit there and look pretty. They adapt. They survive droughts, push through cracks in concrete and reach for light even when it seems out of reach. They thrive despite the odds – and so do you.

This journey wasn't just about growing plants. It was about growing yourself.

So go, keep building your jungle. Keep pushing boundaries. Keep learning, experimenting and sharing your passion. And when your friends inevitably ask how the hell you keep your plants alive? Smile, lean back and say – 'Because I'm a Jungle Boss, mate.'

And remember – if you ever feel lost, I'm here. You're part of something now – a wild, wonderful community of fellow plantaholics who know that plants aren't just things we care for. They're part of who we are.

Thanks for letting me be a part of your journey, you absolute legend.

Go forth and turn the world green!

*One Love,
Tiny
Phone People*

ACKNOWLEDGEMENTS

Writing this book has been like propagating a stubborn cutting – slow, messy, often unsure of what I was doing – but look, it rooted. It rooted because of love, patience, and the strange magic of people who keep showing up for you, even when your house looks like a jungle and you start talking to plants more than humans.

To Charlotte – my compass, my co-pilot and the better half of this operation. You've packed more plants than I can count, picked up the pieces when I dropped the ball, and reminded me why it's all worth it. You are the soil that holds this whole wild mess together.

To my children: Tallulah, my spark of wonder and adventure, who looks at life like it's one big greenhouse of possibilities, and Phoenix, my quiet strength, whose steady presence keeps me grounded like a well-rooted tree. You both show me every day what it means to grow something real.

To Mum and Dad – Pam and Frank. You gave me my roots. You taught me how to work hard, think big, and never take life too seriously. From steel welding to storytelling, you've supported every turn this journey's taken, and I carry your strength with me always.

To Mo – my botanical brother from another life. You've stood by me through every wild idea, every dodgy plant haul, and every ridiculous vision we somehow made real. Your generosity and passion breathe life into this community.

To the inner circle of glorious reprobates – Alice, Annie, Sarah, Ben and Kristian. You are the tonic to my madness, the jungle gang that's always got a spare hand, a spare joke or a spare drink. You've kept me laughing, rooted and (mostly) sane.

To every one of you who's been part of this journey – whether you've joined a workshop, sent a kind message, shared a reel or just believed in this beardy bloke with a watering can – thank you. I wish I could name you all, but you know who you are. You've been my rocks, my mirrors and my people. I wouldn't be here without you.

To Crispy, Emily and Oscar – my dream team. You believed in my madness, supported me through the chaos and helped shape this strange, beautiful thing into something magical. Crispy, may married life be filled with joy, laughter and not too many plant murders. Em, may motherhood bring you as much wonder and love as you've poured into these pages. And Oscar – new home, future family and success in everything you touch ... may it all grow wild and true.

To Dave (Big D) – thank you for putting this book together so beautifully and somehow bottling the absolute madness of my DNA in printed form. From watching you on *The Mighty Boosh* to actually working with you? That's a timeline twist I never saw coming. You made it unique. You made it me. Love you, bro.

To Jade – part plant-sitter, part chaos buddy and very much the annoying little sister I never asked for but clearly needed. Without you, half my collection would be crispy compost by now. Thank you for always being up for a mission, sista. You're a legend (even if you do water like you're in an action film).

And to my haters, doubters, and professional complainers – thank you, sincerely. Life needs balance: yin and yang, light and shade, chlorophyll and spider mites ... and then there's you, the mildew on the leaf of motivation. The more you doubt me, the further I go. You're like the fertiliser I didn't ask for but accidentally spilled – stinky, but strangely effective. Keep doing your thing. I'll keep doing mine – louder, greener, and with significantly better lighting.

Lastly, to the plants – yes, you. The divas, the creepers, the ones who died tragically and the ones who lived in spite of me. You've taught me everything worth knowing: patience, presence, and how life always finds a way to grow again.

One love, always.

Jonny

INDEX

A
abscisic acid 173
Acacia tortilis 208
aerial roots 51, 203, 213
African violets 62, 120
agaves 53
Aglaonema spp. (Chinese evergreen) 25
    A. 'Silver Bay' 74
    and light 35
air layering 76, 79
air plants 115
air quality 88. *see also* humidity
air stones 160
airflow 24, 88, 91, 94, 96
Alocasia 18, 145
    A. 'Loco' 160
    A. micholitziana 'Frydek' Variegata 155
    A. 'Polly' 25
    and humidity 43
    and pests 71
    seasonal changes 105
    soil mix 52
    and stress 97
aloe vera 53, 114
Anthurium 20
    A. andraeanum 113
    A. clarinervium 25
    A. forgetii 153
    A. forgetii x nigrolaminum 'Gigi' 115
    A. veitchii 112
    A. warocqueanum 112
    and humidity 43, 86, 90, 112
    and light 33
    seasonal changes 105
    soil mix 50
aphids 68, 70, 95
Aroids
    and humidity 90, 113
    soil mix 49, 129, 153
artificial light 36, 37
Aspidistra (cast-iron plant) 25, 37, *172*
    and pests 71
    seasonal changes 105
auxins 173, 193

B
bark mix 160
basil: pruning 120
Begonia
    B. maculata 26
    B. pavonina (peacock begonia) 153
    and humidity 90
bird of paradise 79, 144, 145
bonsai 120, 121
Boston ferns 52, 62, 113
bottom planting 145
bottom watering 41, 42
bulbophyllums 112
buying plants 23–7

C
cacti
    and humidity 86, 114
    and light 33
    soil mix 53
    watering 44
Calathea 18
    C. 'Medallion' 25
    and humidity 86, 90, 94
    and light 33
    and pests 71
    soil mix 52
    and stress 97
    watering 42
calcium 60, 136, 209
Cape sundew 115, 208
carnivorous plants 115, 208
cast-iron plant 25, 37, *172*
    and pests 71
    seasonal changes 105
charcoal 49, *52*, 78, 160
Chinese evergreen 25, 35, 74
chlorophyll 60, 178
chloroplasts 195
chodes 77
choosing plants 23–7
citrus trees 33, 62
cleaning 88
climbing plants 119, 121–3
coconut coir 136
coleus: pruning 120
communication 185–9, 208, 211
compost *51*, 136
containers 137, 145
Croton 33, 37
cuttings 76–81
cytokinins 173

D
dehydration 94
Dendrophylax lindenii (ghost orchid) 187
Dieffenbachia 144
diseases 88, 120, 128. *see also* fungal growth; pests
displays 143–7
distilled water 42, 86, 115
division 76
dormancy 42, 61, 105, 201, 203
Dracaena
    fertilising 62
    statement plants 144
    and stress 97
    watering 44
Drosera capensis (Cape sundew) 115, 208
dry air 42, 43. *see also* humidity

E
Echeveria 79, 114
environment 95, 96, 101–7. *see also* airflow; humidity
epigenetics 209
epiphytes 115
    ghost orchid 187

Epipremnum 51, 121
   E. albo variegata 102
   E. pinnatum 'Cebu Blue' 20
espalier 121
ethylene 173

F

ferns 145
   Boston ferns 52, 62, 113
   fertilising 62
   and humidity 43, 86, 87, 90, 112, 113
   and light 35
   maidenhair ferns 71, 113
   and pests 71
   propagation 76
   pruning 120
   seasonal changes 105
   soil mix 52
   and stress 97
fertilisers 59–63
   choosing 60, 95
   natural 136
   over-fertilisation 61
   seasonal changes 61, 104
   and sustainability 136
   types of 62–3
fibrous roots 195
Ficus 120, 208
   F. elastica 37, 120
   F. elastica 'Shivereana' 26
fiddle-leaf figs 144, 145
   leaf drop 94
   propagation 76, 79
   and stress 97
finger test 17, 41
fish tank propagation 77
fish tank water 77, 136
fittonias 42, 112, 145
fungal growth 49, 88
fungi and plant communication 185
fungus gnats 68–9

G

gibberellins 173
grouping plants 87, 137
grow lights 36, 37, 102
growth 191–7

H

hanging plant displays 145
Haworthia 114
Hibiscus 62
hormones 173, 209
horticultural grit 53
houseplants. *see* plants
Hoya 37, 90, 121
humidifiers 86, 90
humidity 24, 42, 43, 85–91
   controlling 86–7, 90, 96
   levels of 86
   misting 42, 86, 113, 115
   seasonal changes 104
   signs of 94
   speciality plants 112
hydration. *see* watering
hydrophobic soil 128

I

intelligence 211
iron 60
ivy 121, 145

J

jade plants 20, 79, 114
jade trees 120

L

labels 16–17
ladybugs 70
lavender 71
leaves 195. *see also*
   photosynthesis
   leaf cuttings 76
   signs of stress 94
   tannin secretion 208
   variegation 177, 178, 195
LECA balls 51, 78
light 24, 31–9
   artificial 36, 37
   bright, direct light 33, 37
   bright, indirect light 33, 37
   grow lights 36, 37, 102
   imbalance of 95, 172, 193
   low light 17, 35, 37
   medium light 35, 37
   and plant displays 144
   reflectors and mirrors 35
   seasonal changes 102
   sky test 33
looking after plants 18–20, 24

M

magnesium 60
maidenhair ferns 71, 113
masdevallias 112
mealybugs 68
memory 208–9
meristems 193
microclimates
   grouping plants 87, 137
   and humidity 87, 90
   in your home 24
Mimosa pudica 208
mint 71
mirrors 35
mislabelled plants 17
misting 42, 86, 113, 115
Monstera
   fertilising 62
   and humidity 86, 113
   and light 33
   M. 'Albo' 178
   M. deliciosa 20, 26, *105*, 153
   M. deliciosa 'Aurea Variegata' *153*
   M. esqueleto 152
   M. obliqua 76
   M. 'Peru' 26
   M. pinnatipartita 61, 95
   Monstera Thai Constellation 179, 201
   mutations 179
   and pests 71
   propagation 76, 79
   pruning 120
   seasonal changes 105
   soil mix 51

statement plants 144
and stress 97
training 121
watering 42, 44
mosses 112, 145
mould 88
mutation 177–80

N

names of plants 17
neem oil 70
nematodes 70
Neptunia oleracea 208
nitrogen 60
nutrients 59–63, 95, 172
  distribution of 172, 185, 187, 195

O

orchids 145, 208
  Dendrophylax lindenii 187
  Dracula orchids 112
  ghost orchid 187
  and humidity 87, 90, 112
  jewel orchids 112
  pruning 120
  soil mix 50
overwatering 41, 94, 95, 195

P

palms 62
peace lilies
  fertilising 62
  and humidity 90, 113
  and light 35
  propagation 76, 79
  pruning 120
  soil mix 52
  watering 42, 44
peacock begonia 153
peat 136
pebble trays 86
pennywort 44
Peperomia 42, 145
perlite 50, 78, 160

pesticides 70, 138
pests 67–73
  and airflow 88
  controlling 70, 95, 138
  and plant types 71
  signs of 94, 95
  sustainable control 138
  types of 68–9
Philodendron 144, 208
  fertilising 62
  and humidity 87, 90, 113
  and light 33
  P. burle marxii Variegata 97
  P. giganteum 59
  P. gloriosum 26
  P. spiritus sancti 152
  and pests 71
  'Pink Princess' 178, 201
  propagation 76, 79
  pruning 120
  seasonal changes 105
  soil mix 51
  and stress 97
  training 121
  watering 42, 44
phloem 172
phosphorous 60
photosynthesis 33, 76, 172. *see also* light
pine bark 50, 78
pitcher plants 115
plant care
  approaches to 18–20
  environment 95–6, 101–7
  four pillars of 24
  mutations 179
  rare plants 151–5
  rehabilitation 159–65
  seasonal 101–7
  speciality plants 111–17
  and sustainability 135–41
plant communication 185–9, 208, 211
plant hormones 173, 209
plant intelligence 211
plant memory 208–9
plant names 17

plant science 171–5
plant stress 93–9, 208–9
plants
  adaptability of 200–5
  choosing 23–7
  cleaning 88
  dramatic 25
  fast-growing 26
  history of 199–200
  labels 16–17
  resilient 25
  sentience 207–13
  unusual 26
plastic pots 137
potassium 60
Pothos
  fertilising 62
  golden pothos 20
  and humidity 86, 87, 90
  and light 35
  mutations 179
  propagation 76, 79
  pruning 120
  seasonal changes 105
  and stress 97
  training 121
  watering 44
pots 137
predator mites 70, 138
propagation 75–81
  methods 76–7
  propagation boxes 78, 87
  and sustainability 138
  water propagation 161
pruning 119–23, 193

R

rainwater 42
rare plants 151–5
reflectors 35
rehabilitation 159–65
repotting 127–33
Rhaphidophora 51, 113
  R. tetrasperma 25, *122*
root diagnosis test 130
root rot 160, 161, 195
roots 127–33

aerial 51, 203, 213
fibrous 195
nutrient distribution 172, 185, 187, 195
repotting 127–9
taproots 195
rosemary 71
rubber plants
fertilising 62
and humidity 86, 87, 90
and pests 71
propagation 76, 79
pruning 120
and stress 97

S

sand *53*
Sansevieria (snake plants) 18, *35*, *103*
and humidity 90
and light 35
and pests 71
propagation 76, 79
seasonal changes 105
soil mix 53
and stress 97
watering 44
scale 68
Scindapsus pictus 178
seasonal changes 42, 101–7
sentience 207–13
snake plants 18, *35*, *103*
and humidity 90
and light 35
and pests 71
propagation 76, 79
seasonal changes 105
soil mix 53
and stress 97
watering 44
soaking plants 42
soil 24, 47–54. *see also*
fertilisers
and charcoal 49
function of 48
hydrophobic 128
living soil mix 61, 62, 187

propagation mix 78
soil mixes 48–9, 50–3
and sustainability 136
Spathiphyllum aurea 91
speciality plants 111–17
sphagnum moss *52*, 78, 160
spider mites 68
spider plants 20
fertilising 62
and humidity 90
and light 35
and stress 97
watering 44
statement plants 144
stem cuttings 76
stomata 195
stressed plants 93–9, 208–9
stunted growth 94
succulents 17, 37
and humidity 86, 114
and light 33
overwatering 203
propagation 76
soil mix 53
sundews 115, 208
sustainability 135–41
Syngonium 51, 113, 179
S. 'Albo' 26
S. 'Mojito' *113*

T

taproots 195
temperature swings 95, 102
terrariums 112, 145
thrips 68
Tillandsia 115
tissue culture mutations 179
training plants 121–3

U

underwatering 41, 94, 95

V

variegation 177, 178, 195
ventilation 24, 88, 91, 94, 95, 96

Venus flytraps 115
vermiculite *52*, 78

W

water propagation 161
watering 24, 40–5
bottom watering 41, 42
deep watering 42
finger test 17, 41
and growth 193
overwatering 41, 94, 95, 195
rainwater 42
seasonal changes 42, 103
and sustainability 137
techniques 42
underwatering 41, 94, 95
water quality 42
weekly 17
'weight test' 95
'weight test' 95
wilting 94
Wood Wide Web 172, 185, 211
worm castings *50*, 78

X

xylem 172

Y

yuccas 53

Z

ZZ plants 18
and light 35
and pests 71
propagation 76, 79
seasonal changes 105
and stress 97
watering 44, 200

EBURY PRESS

UK | USA | Canada | Ireland | Australia
India | New Zealand | South Africa

Ebury Press is part of the Penguin Random House group of companies whose addresses can be found at global.penguinrandomhouse.com

Penguin Random House UK
One Embassy Gardens, 8 Viaduct Gardens, London SW11 7BW

penguin.co.uk

global.penguinrandomhouse.com

First published by Ebury Press in 2026

1

Copyright © Jonny Balchandani 2026

Photography © Dave Brown 2026 except for the below

Top-left image on page 44 © Adobe Stock 2026

The moral right of the author has been asserted.

No part of this book may be used or reproduced in any manner for the purpose of training artificial intelligence technologies or systems. In accordance with Article 4(3) of the DSM Directive 2019/790, Penguin Random House expressly reserves this work from the text and data mining exception.

Editorial Director: Sam Crisp

Senior Editor: Emily Brickell

Senior Production Manager: Lucy Harrison

Design and Photography: Dave Brown apeinc.co.uk / davebrown.photo

Illustration: Ivana Zorn

Colour origination by Altaimage Ltd
Printed and bound in China by C&C Offset Printing Co., Ltd.

The authorised representative in the EEA is Penguin Random House Ireland, Morrison Chambers, 32 Nassau Street, Dublin D02 YH68.

A CIP catalogue record for this book is available from the British Library

ISBN 9781529956467

Penguin Random House is committed to a sustainable future for our business, our readers and our planet. This book is made from Forest Stewardship Council® certified paper.